UML™:
A Beginner's Guide

Jason T. Roff

McGraw-Hill/Osborne

New York   Chicago   San Francisco
Lisbon   London   Madrid   Mexico City
Milan   New Delhi   San Juan
Seoul   Singapore   Sydney   Toronto

The McGraw·Hill Companies

McGraw-Hill/Osborne
2600 Tenth Street
Berkeley, California 94710
U.S.A.

To arrange bulk purchase discounts for sales promotions, premiums, or fund-raisers, please contact **McGraw-Hill**/Osborne at the above address. For information on translations or book distributors outside the U.S.A., please see the International Contact Information page immediately following the index of this book.

UML™: A Beginner's Guide

    67890 FGR FGR 0198765

ISBN 0-07-222460-6

Publisher   Brandon A. Nordin
Vice President & Associate Publisher   Scott Rogers
Acquisitions Editor   Lisa McClain
Project Editor   Janet Walden
Acquisitions Coordinator   Athena Honore
Technical Editor   Alexander Vendrov
Copy Editor   William McManus
Proofreader   Karen Mead
Indexer   David Heiret
Computer Designers   Carie Abrew, Tabitha M. Cagan
Illustrators   Michael Mueller, Lyssa Wald, Melinda Moore Lytle
Series Design   Jean Butterfield
Cover Series Design   Sarah F. Hinks

This book was composed with Corel VENTURA™ Publisher.

For Zachary, I love you.
For Kimberly, I love you.

About the Author

Jason T. Roff owns and operates First Factory, Inc., a software development consulting firm specializing in Microsoft software and Internet development, documentation services, and web hosting (www.firstfactoryinc.com).

Jason has written a handful of books on database development and e-commerce careers and currently specializes in .NET development with SQL Server and offsite project management. Jason received his B.S. from Albany University in Computer Science with Applied Mathematics and is currently seeking his M.S. degree.

Jason lives happily in Long Island, NY with his wife Kimberly and son Zachary. Jason can be reached at jason@firstfactoryinc.com. Feel free to drop by.

Contents at a Glance

Contents

Acknowledgments

There are so many people I would like to thank for the complete fulfillment of this book and its future success. To start off, I would like to thank McGraw-Hill/Osborne as a whole for their continued support. All the authors and potential authors out there should pay attention—this is the place to write for. They really have their act together, and that means a lot.

And for all the authors and potential authors out there who want to work and write for the best publishers, I recommend that you contact David Fugate of Waterside Productions, Inc. (www.waterside.com). David is my agent. Most people think of the word "agent" and relate it to either Jerry Maguire or Hollywood. Although David lives in California, he is not your typical agent. He is down-to-earth and a great guy just to bounce ideas and questions off of. I thank David very much for getting me this project and for helping me complete it.

My editors have been excellent throughout the entire process. I have so many of them to thank. Ann Sellers had a lot of faith in me and stuck by me on a lot of points and I want to thank her for that. Lisa McClain continued that support when I needed it and she deserves the same level of thanks. Timothy Madrid, Janet Walden, and Bill McManus worked very closely with me, watching my every detail, and seemed always to know the answers to my questions.

My technical editor, Alexander Vendrov, has been wonderful. This man has more knowledge about the UML specification and its application than anybody I know. I strongly believe that this knowledge is reflected in this book and that you will benefit from it as much as I have. I hope to work with Alex again in the future.

And, of course, there is the other Alex. Alexander Petrov has been a friend to me for many years now. Sometimes it is technical, sometimes it is for a laugh, but whenever the time and whatever the reason, he has always come through for me. Thank you Alex…here is to many more years.

My wife, Kimberly, has put up with so much more than she has deserved to. She listens to me when I talk technical and she allows me to miss events so that I can get my work done. I love my wife and thank her for everything I have.

My son, Zachary, is almost two years old and has been the reason I continue to write, work, and learn. I have to keep up with him. I love you, son.

–Jason

Introduction

The Unified Modeling Language is a bear to understand for any beginner. There are many resources available for developers to use if they know UML and need to learn how to apply it, or if they want to know more about what they already have a foundation for. This book was written to fill this gap and provide real beginners with the understanding and foundation that are required to effectively learn UML and apply it toward modeling the systems that they are tasked to create.

Who Should Read this Book

This book was written for developers, analysts, quality assurance people, and project managers. Do not be mislead by the title of this book. Although UML topics are covered for people from the beginner stage, this book is not only for beginner developers or entry-level analysts. In fact, this book assumes that you have a basic understanding of what software is and how it is generally built.

Analysts will walk away from this book with an understanding of how to obtain business requirements from users or potential users of a system. They will learn and understand what the developers need in order to write a system. Developers will learn how to use the information provided by the analysts to begin modeling the specifics of their system and ultimately code it. Quality assurance people will learn how to read the blueprints of the applications that they test so that they can be more effective in their job. Project managers, of course, can learn how to oversee the entire process so that the project runs smoothly.

If you are reading this far, you probably already share the understanding that software should be modeled before it is developed. You may be lucky enough to be learning this before working on any major project, or you may be reading this book because you are currently working on one. Regardless, it is never too late to learn how to do something right, and this book will show you.

What this Book Covers

This book covers UML in a progressive order, beginning with analysis, through construction, and on to deployment.

Module 1, "UML Fundamentals," introduces the concept of the Unified Modeling Language to you as you learn why you should model software before you dive into development. Through a discussion of the origins of UML, including who created it and for what reason, you will be introduced to the different pieces of UML and the Unified Process, the method through which you can utilize UML to model your systems.

Module 2, "Use Case Diagrams," teaches you how to interrogate a domain expert (the person who will become the superuser of your eventually developed system) to identify the parameters of the system you will model. This module shows you how to take this information and formulate it into use cases, which are considered the building blocks of any system model.

Module 3, "Introduction to Object-Oriented Design," gives you a brief introduction to object-oriented concepts as they pertain to the modeling process. UML was designed to work for object-oriented design (OOD), which therefore requires a solid understanding.

Module 4, "Workflow Modeling with Activity Diagrams," illustrates how activity diagrams become the next logical step, after use case diagrams, when modeling your system because they depict the path in which the user travels in order to complete a use case.

Module 5, "Modeling Behavior with Sequence Diagrams," builds on your knowledge from the previous module and activity diagram modeling with an alternative diagram, the sequence diagram. This module explains the differences between the two diagrams and gives examples of when to use each.

Module 6, "Defining Domain Models Using Class Diagrams," is an introduction to class diagrams as they are used to define the basic building blocks of your design that you will embellish later.

Module 7, "Collaboration Diagrams," shows how you can combine class diagrams with sequence diagrams to explain how objects communicate with each other in the message flow that you have already dictated in your sequence diagrams.

Module 8, "Further Explanation of Class Diagrams," introduces more features of the class diagram to use when you begin designing your system, rather than analyzing it. As you will learn, UML is best when used iteratively, and class diagrams are one of the diagrams that can be used at different levels of your modeling.

Module 9, "Further Explanation of Sequence Diagramming," goes into even more depth about sequence diagramming as you are working more and more with the design of your system rather than with the analysis of it.

Module 10, "Modeling Behavior with Statechart Diagrams," takes a look at the statechart diagram and how it is used to model the current state of a system. In this module, you will learn about actions, events, and composite states.

Module 11, "Architecting with Implementation Diagrams," shows the use of the two implementation diagrams, deployment and component. The two diagrams are used together in many situations to illustrate where pieces of software are being distributed.

Module 12, "Using the Object Constraint Language," is a brief introduction to UML's language for specifying constraints. This module explains how you can populate your diagram with OCL to specify business constraints that would restrict flows, trigger events, and guard actions.

Appendix A, "Answers to Mastery Checks," gives the answers to all of the mastery check questions presented in the 12 modules.

And finally, the Glossary provides an easy reference for most of the UML and OCL terms used in this book.

How to Read this Book

This book was written to be read from cover to cover while referencing the glossary and the mastery check answers at the end of the book. If you are only interested in the analysis side of modeling with UML, you can focus your attention on Modules 1 through 4. However, anybody else involved in the modeling tasks for construction (development) should read the entire book.

Even if you are only interested in the analysis, learning how a developer will design the applications from your models is important. To understand how somebody else will interpret your work and carry it on to the next step will definitely shape how you prepare your own work.

Special Features

Almost every module contains hints, tips, and notes to help you understand UML. Each module in this book contains many UML diagrams that have been meticulously created to help you learn the current topic. Some modules contain Ask the Expert question-and-answer sections to provide even more additional information that may not be easily inferred from the direct reading of this book.

Each module contains step-by-step projects that walk you through, while pacing your knowledge of, the module's topic. Most modules that introduce a new diagram contain at least one project that helps you read a sample UML diagram after you have learned the notation for it. Most of these modules also contain a project that helps you model the given UML diagram after the steps for modeling the diagram have been discussed in that module. To assist you in the projects, answers to each step can be found online at www.osborne.com and www.firstfactoryinc.com.

While writing this book, I have continually found that the UML specification is not only dry but also very difficult to understand. I have made every effort possible to convey this information to you in the most upbeat fashion with both light-hearted and realistic examples. I hope you get as much enjoyment out of reading this book as I have had writing it.

Module 1

UML Fundamentals

No activities so influence the quality of a product as do architecture and design

–James O. Coplien, AT&T Bell Laboratories

One of the questions that most novice developers ask is, why do I need to model software? This question is asked all the time because very rarely are developers taught to model before they are taught to code, especially if they are self taught. In fact, most developers became developers from monkeying around in code. Their amazement at what they could achieve soon grew into a skill. This skill has become, for most self-taught developers, the only conceivable way of building a system. This book, specifically this module, will help you realize how great your systems can become with a little modeling.

Learn Why We Model Software

The most important reason we model software is to achieve a high level of quality from our finished product. A well-architected product will pay off in the end—you've heard it before, but you just don't know how or why. High quality doesn't just happen; there are a number of things that occur in between the stages of conception and a finished product that are direct results of modeling prior to development. High quality is a product of ease of development, shorter development cycles, better user documentation and less bugs through better testing.

It is a fact that good structure will last and poor structure will fail. A product that has been built on a good foundation, with consistent methods of achieving goals, plenty of reuse, and bug-free code, is no sweat to fix—especially by the people who built it.

Take, for example, Legos. I'm sure you've played with these at least once in your life. If you remember correctly (or if you have kids—if you are doing it now), there are very few restrictions as to how Legos can go together. You can put bricks on top of the little people's heads just as easily as you can put a roof on four walls. Software is like this. In most cases, you can write code with very few restrictions.

If you also remember, all Lego sets are meant to build a particular structure, whether it be a house, space station, hospital, or castle. Have you ever tried to build one of these things from sight? Have you ever said, "I'm going to build a castle with these Legos," and then just started building? Many new software developers do just this. They say "Hey! I know how to write software. I know how to put Legos together. I can build a system!" Their intentions are good, but their technique needs some work.

Now, do you remember that 20-page document inside the box of Legos that showed you step by step exactly how to build the castle? How much easier was it then? It probably took you very little time to follow the directions to build the final product. I'll even guarantee you that it took you far less time to follow the directions to build the castle than it took for somebody to come up with the directions in the first place. I'll even guarantee you that it takes less time to make the instructions to build the castle and then to follow the instructions to build the castle than it would take to start from scratch and to build the castle without any directions at all.

It is a fact that software modeling takes longer than development. It is a fact that development time can be drastically reduced by proper software modeling and documenting.

Analysis, Design, and Implementation

No matter how you slice it, there are three steps to creating a quality system: analysis, design, and implementation. I like to think that a successful project is the result of a lot of analysis, less design, and even less implementation, because it is true that if you have the exact opposite order, you will have a complete nightmare on your hands. A lot of implementation with little design and even less analysis usually results in a product that is first riddled with bugs, and then doesn't have the functionality that users require.

Figure 1-1 shows you six possible scenarios when developing a system. The first is ideal, while the rest are just different ways of screwing it up.

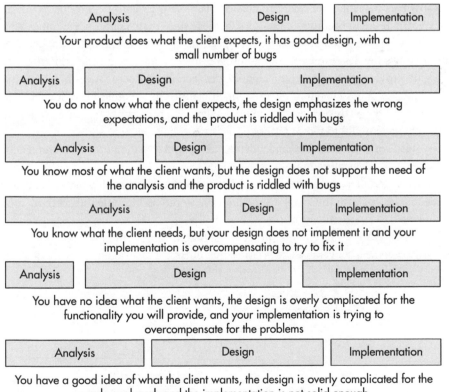

Figure 1-1 Different doses of analysis, design, and implementation

During the analysis phase, you would consult a domain expert. A domain expert is a person who is considered to be an authority on the system you will be creating. For example, if you needed to create an airline ticket-entry system, who would you consider your domain experts? Would it be the airline company, the ticketing agents, or the passengers? To answer this, you need to ask yourself, who will use the system? A ticketing agent would likely use an airline ticket-entry system.

Software Lifecycle Models

There are three very common software lifecycle models that have been around for years: waterfall, spiral (or iterative), and incremental-iterative. The waterfall method, shown in Figure 1-2, is straightforward. You start with analysis, then you design, and then you develop.

The waterfall method is probably the most commonly used lifecycle approach, because it is the closest to common sense—it comes more naturally to people than the other two approaches. The spiral, or iterative, software lifecycle model, shown in Figure 1-3, is a little different in that it involves repeating the waterfall method over and over until the product is done.

As you can see in Figure 1-3, the spiral process starts with analysis, continues with design, follows up with implementation, and then repeats itself by returning to the analysis phase. This method allows the development team to progressively complete a project. Perhaps the first phase only provides must-have functionality, the second adds some nice-to-have features, and the final pass includes far-out never-used functionality. On the other hand, it could take several passes through the analysis, design, and implementation phases before you have anything that is remotely meaningful to the end user.

The third software lifecycle model that is very popular is the iterative-incremental method (see Figure 1-4). Basically, this approach divides a project into subprojects, and allows you to perform the waterfall method on each. Instead of completing functionality in the entire application with each pass, as with the iterative method, the iterative-incremental method completes components based upon functionality with each phase.

With the iterative-incremental process approach, each completed component does not necessarily become a deliverable that is usable by a client. At milestones, however, the components

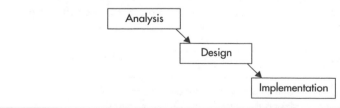

Figure 1-2 The waterfall software lifecycle model

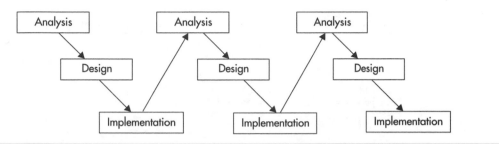

Figure 1-3 The spiral software lifecycle model

can be joined to create a usable product. This method is preferred because it promotes a high return of reusable code. By separating your functionality into different components, such as data access, business logic, and GUI controls, you know exactly where the functionality you want is.

Progress Check

1. What are the elements that make quality systems?

2. Who would be the domain expert for a railroad kiosk?

3. Describe the incremental-iterative development model?

Understand the Unified Modeling Process

The Unified Modeling Language is only a language. It is not a way of designing a system, but it is a way to model a system. To use UML, you need to apply a method to it. There are a number of methods that have been designed, but the most popular, and probably the first to deal with UML, is the Rational Unified Process (RUP), also called the Unified Process.

---

1. Ease of development, shorter development cycles, better user documentation, and less bugs through better testing.

2. Train passengers would be a good source of information to learn what they want to see. However, the railroad would be able to tell you what was available to show them.

3. During the initial phase of analysis, design, and implementation, the system is divided into components, each of which has its own analysis, design, and implementation phases.

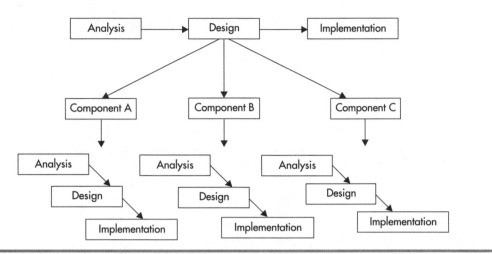

Figure 1-4 The iterative software lifecycle model

I could teach you the UML notation, but doing so won't help you to understand how to apply it to your system design. Therefore, I will be using a loose interpretation of the Unified Process to teach UML. If you work at a company that is using UML strictly already, then chances are it strictly enforces RUP, with diagrams on the doors that have been sent along with the Rational Rose product from Rational Software. If you are bringing UML to your company, chances are you will be experimenting with your new knowledge, teaching others how UML can fit into your existing business operations rather than showing your boss how to change everything to fit the Unified Process.

Simply stated, this process is not carved in stone. In fact, you should adapt it to your needs and your skills. You will find that you can easily cut corners with a lot of the specifics, but in some cases, you will also find that you need much more than RUP has to offer. This is where evolution will kick in and allow you to change your process until it fits your situation quite well.

TIP

Three other processes are Object-Oriented Software Process (OOSP), OPEN Process (www.open.org.au), and ICONIX Unified Object Modeling (www.iconixsw.com/Spec_Sheets/UnifiedOM.html).

The Unified Process has its roots in Ivar Jacobson's Objectory organization, which was merged with Rational. The process, Objectory Process, was enhanced with Rational's own process and released as the Unified Process in December 1998.

A software development process is a set of phases that are followed to bring a product, or a system, from conception to delivery. In the Unified Process, there are four of these phases:

- **Inception** Identify the system you are going to develop, including what it contains and its business case.

- **Elaboration** Perform detailed design and identify the foundation of your system.

- **Construction** Write the software.

- **Transition** Deliver the system to the users—sometimes better known as *rolling out* the system.

Inception Phase

The inception phase of the Unified Process is where you do your initial analysis. You discuss with the software matter expert (or domain expert) what the system you will be designing should do. In this stage, the business requirements need to be identified, fleshed out, and modeled in use case diagrams. Module 2 deals specifically with this phase of the Unified Process. Module 10 helps you to model the business flow of more complex systems.

Elaboration Phase

The elaboration phase of the Unified Process is the phase in which the design takes place. From the use cases, the design team works to get a unified image of how the system should be constructed. The design team will continue to iteratively pare down the system into subsystems, each of which can be modeled separately. This is no easy task, which is why we have dedicated a large portion of this book to the design of a system.

During the elaboration phase, you will evolve the use cases discovered in the inception phase into a design of the domain, its subsystems, and the business objects related to it. From there, you will iteratively turn this domain model into a software design using more detailed diagrams that will eventually model classes and their members.

This book focuses very heavily upon the elaboration phase of the Unified Process, leveraging object-oriented design and analysis and UML to prepare your team to construct a product based upon a well-thought-out design.

Construction Phase

The construction phase of the Unified Process is the actual building of the product from the design of the system. In the Unified Process, the development portion is an incremental iterative process. Code will be developed in portions that are manageable. Each portion will go through minicycles similar to the entire Unified Process. The construction phase will call for changes to the design and questions for the analysis. You must be flexible enough in your approach to continue, but you also must be firm in your stance so that project creep does not occur.

You will find yourself consistently going back to previous phases, particularly the elaboration phase, to design new components that may not have been realized earlier in the modeling process. This will happen especially in the iterative-incremental software lifecycle model discussed earlier.

Transition Phase

The transition phase is a little outside of the scope of this book. It deals with delivering the product to customers, perhaps a beta site or even the actual client. If you've developed software before, you know that this is not the real end of the software lifecycle—not by far. Constant maintenance and upgrades usually follow the successful (and even unsuccessful) "completion" of a software product. At the very end, there is the twilight phase—the phase where the product gets phased out of existence.

Progress Check

1. What is done during the inception phase of the Unified Process?

2. What is done during the elaboration phase of the Unified Process?

3. What is done during the construction phase of the Unified Process?

CRITICAL SKILL
1.3 Gain an Understanding of What UML Is

The Unified Modeling Language is a notation and a semantic language that can be applied to any software development process. Primarily, Rational Software and its three superstars, Grady Booch, Jim Rumbaugh, and Ivar Jacobson, developed UML. This notation combines the best of the best from these three designers, resulting in a standard that has international support. UML uses several types of diagrams, all of which can be used to model object-oriented software systems.

---

1. Analysis
2. Design
3. Implementation

The History

The first two members of the UML dream team, Grady Booch and Jim Rumbaugh, started at Rational creating the new notation in 1994. They offered their own design methods, the Booch method and the Object Modeling Technique (OMT), respectively. In 1995, Dr. Ivar Jacobson joined the team, offering his own method, Object-Oriented Software Engineering (OOSE). Jacobson is commonly known as the father of use cases. Of the three methods, Rumbaugh's OMT has the most prevalent contribution to UML.

The three men set forth on a path to create a unified modeling language because their three individual methods were coming to a point regardless. They all were merging into one set of notation on their own, and they decided to join forces. Doing this allowed them to bring standardization to object modeling.

The first version of UML was UML 0.8. After the first delivery of the UML specification, the three authors requested outside feedback for their work. In 1995, an agreement was made with the Object Management Group (OMG) to make UML a standard. By 1996, outside companies where getting involved in the decision making of how UML would evolve. This resulted in the UML 1.0 standard. In 1997, additional companies joined the forces and helped push out the UML 1.1 response. This book uses the current (as of this writing) version of 1.4, which was approved in 2001. Currently, a new 2.0 version is very close to becoming approved. This book assumes that the current version of the 2.0 RFP will become the official 2.0 specification.

The following companies and individuals have had substantial influence on the design of the UML notation:

- Colorado State University: Robert France

- Computer Associates: John Clark

- Concept 5 Technologies: Ed Seidewitz

- Data Access Corporation: Tom Digre

- Enea Data: Karin Palmkvist

- Hewlett-Packard Company: Martin Griss

- IBM Corporation: Steve Brodsky, Steve Cook

- I-Logix: Eran Gery, David Harel

- ICON Computing: Desmond D'Souza

- IntelliCorp and James Martin & Co.: James Odell

- Kabira Technologies: Conrad Bock

- Klasse Objecten: Jos Warmer

- MCI Systemhouse: Joaquin Miller

- OAO Technology Solutions: Ed Seidewitz

- ObjecTime Limited: John Hogg, Bran Selic

- Oracle Corporation: Guus Ramackers

- PLATINUM Technology Inc.: Dilhar DeSilva

- Rational Software: Grady Booch, Ed Eykholt, Ivar Jacobson, Gunnar Övergaard, Jim Rumbaugh

- SAP: Oliver Wiegert

- SOFTEAM: Philippe Desfray

- Sterling Software: John Cheesman, Keith Short

- Sun Microsystems: Peter Walker

- Telelogic: Cris Kobryn, Morgan Björkander

- Taskon: Trygve Reenskaug

- Unisys Corporation: Sridhar Iyengar, GK Khalsa, Don Baisley

Ask the Expert

Q: **Where are some good places to learn about modeling software?**

A: There are a ton of great places on the Web to find information on modeling software. I'll give you my prime picks.

- **www.uml.org**   Object Management Group, the keepers of UML
- **www.cetus-links.org**   18,309 links on objects and components
- **www.rational.com/uml**   Rational Software's UML page
- **www.sdmagazine.com/uml**   *Software Development Magazine*'s UML Resource Center
- **www.well.com/user/ritchie/oo.html**   The Object-Oriented Page by Ricardo Devis
- **www.uml-zone.com**   DevX's UML Zone

OMG

The Object Management Group (www.omg.org) is a group of over 800 software vendors, developers, and end users dedicated to the promotion of object technology used in developing distributed computing systems. OMG is a nonprofit consortium providing common frameworks for object-oriented applications to build upon.

Progress Check

1. Who were the three major contributors to the UML notation?

2. What organization oversees the UML specification?

3. What is the goal of this organization?

CRITICAL SKILL

1.4 Identify the Pieces of UML

The Unified Modeling Language can be broken into two main pieces—structural diagrams and behavioral diagrams.

Structural Diagrams

UML has two types of diagrams that are considered structural, class diagrams and implementation diagrams. Within these two categories, we can find four specific types of diagrams.

Class and Object Diagram

A class diagram is used to represent the different underlying pieces (classes), their relationship to each other, and which subsystem they belong to. Class diagrams include attributes and operations and well as many types of roles and associations.

An object diagram is very similar to a class diagram, except instead of dealing with classes, it shows objects that are instances of classes. These diagrams are usually more about design by example. In other words, objects deal with individual unique things, whereas classes are more generic.

---

1. Booch, Rumbaugh, and Jacobson
2. Object Management Group (OMG)
3. To standardize object technology for the development of distributed systems

The foundation of any object-oriented system, classes and objects provide management of their own functionality and their data. Classes are used not only to model the domain in early stages of the elaboration phase (as shown in Module 6) but also to build intricate portions of the software design model in later iterations of the same elaboration phase (see Module 8).

UML is used to design systems using object-oriented concepts. Module 3 covers the essentials of being an object-oriented system, including the concept of classes through encapsulation and abstraction, inheritance, and polymorphism. You will learn how to model class diagrams with more detail, applying object-oriented concepts such as multiple and hierarchical inheritance through generalization.

Component and Deployment Diagram

A deployment diagram models where components will wind up after they are installed on systems and how these systems interact with each other. A component diagram is used to illustrate how components of a system interact with each other. It would show dependencies between source files and classes as well as which components they belong to. In the proposed UML 2.0 specification, component diagrams become core functionality, meaning that they become more important in the modeling than they are considered today.

Behavioral Diagrams

Behavioral diagrams are used to show how process flows between components, classes, users, and the system. There are five behavioral diagrams belonging to UML.

Use Case Diagram

Use case diagrams contain use cases and actors, illustrating the relationships between the two sets. Use case diagrams are the starting point of the analysis phase when designing a system. Originally invented by Ivar Jacobson, use cases are the foundation of a use case diagram. They are joined by associations and linked to actors in order to project the overall structure and availability in a system to nontechnical readers such as management and end users. Use cases can be used to diagram the main flow of events in a system, for when there are no errors. They can also be used to diagram alternative flows (related directly to error-handling situations). In Module 2, you will learn by example how to interpret and create use case diagrams based upon user requirements.

Activity Diagram

The activity diagram is used to analyze the behavior within more complex use cases and show their interaction with each other. Activity diagrams are very similar to statechart diagrams insofar as they represent a flow of data; however, activity diagrams are used to model business workflows during the design of use cases. Activity diagrams are usually used to represent the more complicated business activities, helping you identify use cases or the interaction between and within the use cases. Because activity diagrams are used early in the process, we will cover them in Module 4. Statechart diagrams, on the other hand, are used to show how the system changes state and reaches milestones or positions.

Sequence Diagram

The sequence diagram is used to show interaction between actors and objects and other objects. Messages are sent from actor to object, object to object, and object to actor to show the flow of control through a system. Sequence diagrams are used to realize use cases by documenting how a use case is solved with the current design of the system. Sequence diagrams model the interaction between high-level class instances, detailing where process control is at in every stage of the communication process. Sequence diagrams can be used to show every possible path through an interaction, or show a single path through an interaction. Sequence diagrams are covered in Module 5 as they are used to model the domain, and in Module 9 as they are used to design the model.

Collaboration Diagram

Collaboration diagrams are used to bring class diagrams to the next step. They represent the interaction and the relationships between the objects created in earlier steps of your domain modeling process. These diagrams can also be used to model messages between different objects. The navigation of the advanced associations between these objects is explained in the collaboration diagram. Collaboration diagrams are covered in Module 7.

Statechart Diagram

A statechart diagram is used to model the behavior of subsystems, to model the interactions with classes and the system interface, and to realize use cases. Very similar to a well-known state machine model, the statechart diagram is used during the crossover between the analysis and design phases. Statechart diagrams are a wonderful way to visualize the flow of an application. In Module 10, you will learn how to read statechart diagrams and how to create them from complex entities and use cases.

Progress Check

1. What diagram is used to model business requirements?

2. What are the two types of implementation diagrams?

3. What diagram is used to model complex use cases?

Discover Available UML Modeling Tools

A number of modeling tools are available on the market, ranging in price from free to tens of thousands of dollars per seat license. The tool that you will decide to use when modeling a system using UML will depend on your needs, your preferences, and your budget. The list of today's UML modeling tools is very long. In my opinion, two of the most appropriate tools are Rational Rose by Rational Software and Visio by Microsoft, but you cannot discount the tried and trusted whiteboard or a pen and paper.

Rational Rose

Rational Software, being extremely involved in the standardization of UML, and having hired all three of the original contributors, put together one of the first complete UML packages that hit the market. Although pricey in many situations, Rational Rose is an all-in-one package that allows you to reverse engineer your code into models, change your models, and then update your code to reflect the changes. This is called round-trip engineering and is highly promoted in the Rational Rose product.

Rational Rose also has complete object management through a repository of classes and diagrams so that a change in one diagram to a class is easily updated in all the diagrams containing that class. This feature facilitates quicker system design and less mistakes than when using tools that do not consider this information global to the entire system by keeping diagrams unrelated to each other.

Visio

Visio, now owned by Microsoft, has come a long way with the UML functionality it offers. An object manager has been added, which adds component management, just as Rational Rose

---

1. Use case diagram

2. Component and deployment diagrams

3. Activity diagram

offers. The objects (classes, use cases, activities, packages, and so forth) that you create in one diagram can easily be migrated to other diagrams simply by drag and drop.

Although Visio is very comparable to Rational Rose, it is considerably cheaper and allows you to diagram just about anything, from network layouts to office plans, roadmap directions, and project plans. One of the best selling points of Microsoft's Visio is that it is a Microsoft Office component, although it is not usually sold with Microsoft Office. This means that the interface, controls, and functionality are as standard as those in Word and Excel. It is very easy to get up and running with Visio.

Whiteboard or Pen and Paper

And, of course, there are the classics. While you may spend $10,000 on a UML design tool, you will still need a whiteboard, a pen, and some paper. No matter what, you should be using these tools. Use a napkin if you have to, a paper towel, or the back of that telephone bill you keep meaning to pay. These tools are, by far, much easier to use when hashing out ideas as compared to an electronic tool. I find that when I'm on a plane, or watching television, keeping a notebook handy to take notes or scribble ideas is the best way for me to capture my thoughts.

✓ *Module 1 Mastery Check*

1. Why do we model software?

2. What are the three major steps to modeling software?

3. What are the three major software lifecycle models?

4. What are the four phases of the Unified Process?

5. Who are the three major contributors to UML?

6. What was the first version of UML?

7. What does the acronym OMG stand for and what does OMG do?

8. What are the types of structural diagrams within UML?

9. What are the types of behavioral diagrams within UML?

10. What are some tools that can be used to model with UML?

Module 2

Use Case Diagrams

Getting started is the most difficult part of any new process. In software modeling, the first thing you need to do is understand what you are going to model and ultimately develop. As you will learn in this module, use cases are an almost natural point of origin for software design.

2.1 Define Use Case Diagrams

Use case diagrams are the starting point when designing a new system using the Unified Modeling Language. These diagrams originate from the works of Ivar Jacobson in Sweden and are used to enumerate the business requirements of a *system* in ways that everybody involved with the system can understand. Identifying the business requirements for your system is done in the first phase of the Unified Process, inception. From the use case diagrams created in this phase, more diagrams can evolve during the next phase, elaboration.

It might help to understand what a system is, defined in the context of UML. A system is something that does something. It could be a computer application with functions such as printing out your weekly paycheck, or it could be the U.S. government with functions such as passing bills into law. For the purpose of this book, we will stick to computer software, but you should know that UML can be used to model anything that performs a function, such as an automobile, a cell phone, a company, a person's job, or even a person.

A use case diagram is the highest form of detail about a system. It is an excellent way to communicate to management, customers, and other nondevelopment people what a system will do when it is completed. A use case diagram does not go into detail of how a system will do something; this comes later, with future diagrams that are described in this book. A use case diagram does, however, illustrate who will use the system and what they will be able to do with it.

2.2 Discover Why We Model Use Case Diagrams

We model use case diagrams to give ourselves a starting point for designing our system or, sometimes, to describe an existing system. Use case diagrams give us a high-level view of our system, illustrating the functionality that it will provide its users.

Use case diagrams should illustrate to the development team exactly what is expected of an application that they are to develop. It is not unusual for a team outside of development (such as a product management group) to create the use case diagrams. However, more times than not, we find ourselves working on a project with such a small number of people that the

Ask the Expert

Q: **What is the difference between use case diagrams and use cases?**

A: A use case simply describes the actions that users take on a system. A use case diagram includes users, use cases, and the many relationships between the two within a system and possibly one or more subsystems.

development team is forced to play the role of product management and is required to talk to potential users of a system to determine what a system should do.

During this inception phase, we are trying to determine who will use our system and what they will do with it. Once we have gathered this information, we can turn it into use case diagrams and continue on to design so that we can build a system that effectively meets the needs of our newly identified users and requirements. From the use case diagrams, we can determine the interfaces needed between the system and its users.

Use case diagrams are very often produced as a means for illustrating different test cases on a system. Because they are an excellent way to communicate to a user how something is done, they are also a good way to communicate to a tester how a product can be tested.

While use case diagrams can be used to model the normal process flow of a system, they can also be used to model exception processes or error handling functionality. Error handling is a function of an application that is all too often regarded as an afterthought, but with use case diagrams, you can give it the attention it deserves.

Progress Check

1. What should use case diagrams illustrate?

2. In which phase of the Unified Process do use case diagrams first appear?

3. What can be modeled with use case diagrams?

---

1. Business requirements
2. Inception phase
3. Functionality, including tests, normal process flow, and exception process flow

Identify the Notational Components of a Use Case Diagram

Now that we know what a use case diagram is and why we should use one, we should take a look at one.

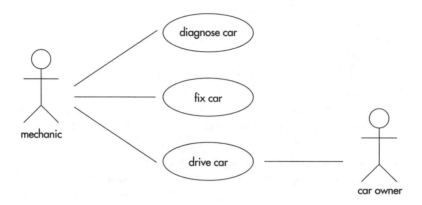

There is not much to a use case diagram. It is pretty straightforward with very few notation components. After a quick glance at the preceding diagram, you should have a fairly good idea of what it represents.

Deconstructing a use case diagram, we find that there are four basic components:

- System
- Actors
- Use cases
- Relationships

While use case diagrams are fairly simple, we'll take the time to explore each of the preceding components to ensure that you understand what they represent.

System

A *system,* as we began to discuss earlier in this module, is something that performs a function. For the purpose of this book, we are interested in computer software, so a system is a piece or multiple pieces of software that performs some sort of function for its users.

In any use case diagram, the actors and use cases shown are part of a single system that is not even identified. It is taken for granted that the system that we are discussing is the system that we are designing and that the use case diagram is part of a bigger modeling solution of a single system.

It is possible for a system to have subsystems, which are organized components within the overall system. Subsystems are discussed in further detail in "Subsystems," later in this module.

Actors

By far the most common notational component of a use case diagram is the *actor*. An actor is used to represent something that uses our system. An actor can be a person or another system. An actor is depicted by a stick figure with the actor's role name listed below it.

When you are naming actors in your use case diagrams, it is important to give them an appropriate name that best describes their function as a user of the system. Avoid giving actors that represent people real people names, such as Jason, Kimberly, or Zachary. Instead, you should name your actors based upon their job title when using the system. For instance, Jason is a developer, Kimberly is a teacher, and Zachary...well, Zachary is a monster.

developer   teacher   monster

When you are constructing your use case diagrams, you want to illustrate every possible actor (user) of your system. If you were to give them all proper names, you would have a lot of work ahead of yourself, trying to list all the developers you knew would use your system (Jason, John, and so on). If you simply list "developer," you would be covered for all of them.

Actors don't necessarily have to be people; they could be other systems that are external to the system that you are modeling.

Use Cases

Use cases are the actions that a user takes on a system. For instance, a developer would create software with a development system, a teacher would record grades with a grading system, and a monster might do a number of different things with some sort of scaring system.

Use cases may be so granular that they cannot contain any other functionality, such as Enter the Letter X, or they may be of a much higher level, such as Type Letters. Sometimes, use cases match up to specific functionality that you would see in the end product, such as the functions that are listed in menu items (such as Print Preview, Page Setup, and Print Document), but more often they are abstract pieces of functionality that are much more general, such as Allow Printing. How the product allows printing is a design technique, not an analysis technique of use case modeling.

The following is an illustration of a few different use cases belonging to the three systems that we described. As you will notice, a use case is illustrated by an oval with a name inside.

You can modify this notation slightly by placing the name of a use case outside the oval, below it. If you decide to use this technique, however, you are strongly urged not to mix it with the previous technique of placing the name of the use case within the oval. By including both notations in the same diagram, you run a high risk of confusing potential readers of the model.

Naming a use case is just as important as naming an actor. Use cases should be text strings, with numbers, letters, and any punctuation except for the colon, which is reserved.

When constructing a use case name, try to use active verbs combined with nouns that describe the functionality being performed on the system; for instance, Crash Car, Lose Money, and Get Insurance.

Having the previous three use cases floating around in the same use case diagram could be very confusing because, as we said earlier, the system is not identified and it is assumed that the diagram depicts use cases of the overall system. It is obvious, however, from reading this module that the use cases Create Software, Record Grades, and Scare Somebody are not part of the same system, or at least not part of the same *package*.

Packages will be discussed in Module 6, but for now I will tell you that a package is a subset of a system that has related functionality. You can identify which package a use case is from by prefixing it with the package name and two colons, such as Development::, Grading::, or Scaring::.

The use of double colons in the package name is the reason why colons are not valid characters to have within a use case name.

Ask the Expert

Q: I know I am allowed to use punctuation in my use case names, but when would I ever want to?

A: There are only a few instances in which I could justify using any sort of punctuation in a use case name:

- If you are using punctuation as a shorthand abbreviation for money, percent, or the word "and," as in Count the $, Calculate % of Return, or Print Documents & Graphs.

- If you (not me) like to avoid using spaces in any string that you write, such as go_home, quit_job, and draw_picture. This is an obvious reference to development languages, which do not allow spaces in variable names. This certainly does not have to be carried over to diagramming—but if you like it, use it.

- If you like to make sure some of your use case names are unique across a large system that others may be using. This is another obvious reference to development, where C/C++ libraries were notorious for using the same technique to make sure that constants would not interfere with constants of an application. Prefixing the name with one or more underscores, such as __run__job, __make__letters, __compile__ program, and __quit__program, accomplishes just this. The thought here is that it is highly unlikely that anybody else would do the same thing.

- If you like to categorize your use cases by type, you could use an identifier in the name, to make it look similar to the Object.Member notation found in object-oriented programming languages, such as Book.Write, Book.Read, and Book.Get. This idea can lead to confusion in your diagrams, especially if you do not practice it throughout your diagrams and start to sway from this technique. It could be argued, however, that when you move to the design stage of your modeling, you can easily map use cases to class functions. However, be warned that it is very unlikely that, this early in the game plan, you will know which objects and which methods you will want or need during design and development. You may find that you are backing yourself into a corner, having to either rework your use case diagrams to rename your use cases or living with the differences and offering a mapping function between the wo so that you know, for example, that the Book.Get use case is handled by the Book.Obtain method. You are better off using Write Book rather than Book.Write, Read Book rather than Book.Read, and Get Book rather than Book.Get.

Relationships

Okay, now onto the meat of use case diagrams, relationships. Relationships are simply illustrated with a line connecting actors to use cases.

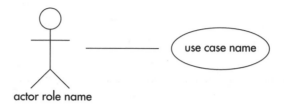

In the example shown in the previous illustration, we see that a developer creates software, a teacher records grades, and a monster scares somebody. Actors can relate to multiple use cases, and use cases can relate to multiple actors, as we see when we begin to expand the grading system, shown here:

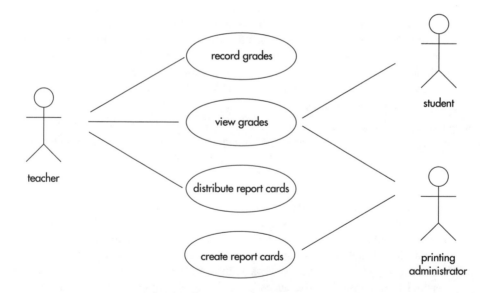

As you can see, we have three actors: a teacher, a student, and a printing administrator. A teacher can record grades, view grades, and distribute report cards. A student can view grades (perhaps through an online program). A printing administrator can create report cards and view grades online to see if the report cards are correct.

As we begin creating relationships between our actors and our use cases, we begin to realize how important it is to choose good names for our actors. Sometimes, a person's title is not a proper name for an actor. A more accurate solution would be to name an actor based upon the role they play in a system—even if that contradicts that user's real-life title. The following illustration depicts poorly chosen actor names.

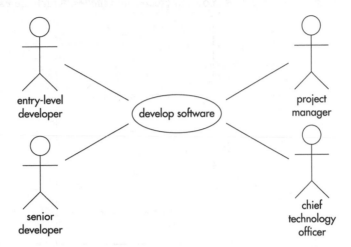

Instead, you would want to generalize the actors' names so that the names better describe the role that the actors play in the system. Instead of listing Entry Level Developer, Senior Developer, Project Manager, and Chief Technology Officer as separate actors, you should simply create one called Developer, because they are using the system to develop software. This name is appropriate even for the chief technology officer—although that person may not be a developer by title, they are developing software when they are using the system.

TIP

If you have more than one actor with the exact same relationships to use cases, as in the previous example, you should reconsider the names you choose for the roles the users play in the system. Consider generalizing the name more and replacing the duplicate actors with a single actor.

Subsystems

Sometimes, you may be modeling a very large system that could benefit from being broken down into more maintainable pieces. You can create such pieces, which are called *subsystems*.

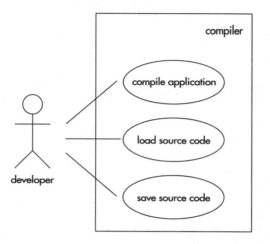

In the preceding example, we see that the developer uses the subsystem, Compiler. Compiler is a subsystem of our overall system, Development Environment. Other subsystems that may be included in the Developer Environment system could be Editor, Debugger, and Source Control.

Progress Check

1. What are the four major components of a use case diagram?

2. What do actors represent?

3. What do use cases represent?

---

1. System, actors, use cases, relationships
2. Users of the system
3. Functions of the system

CRITICAL SKILL
2.4 Understand the Generalization Technique

Generalization is a technique that is used to indicate inheritance of an item in UML. Generalization can be applied to both actors and use cases to indicate that their child items inherit functionality from the parent. Furthermore, this indicates that each child of the parent has slightly different functionality or purpose than the next to warrant its uniqueness.

Use Case to Use Case Relationship

It is easier to understand generalization as it applies to use cases as compared to actors. Take, for instance, this example of an actor that is a system.

This diagram might contradict the earlier tip that when two or more actors are using the same use cases, they should be more generalized to remove the individual actors. However, with generalization this does not apply to this diagram, because although both the developer and the scheduler are compiling the application, they are each doing it differently.

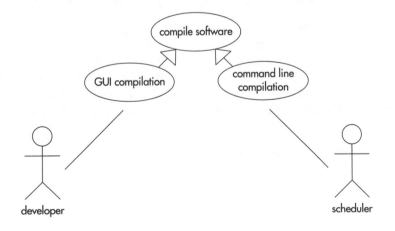

As you can see, the notation for generalization is easy. Each of the two new use cases is a child of the original parent use case. Their notation that relates them to each other is called *generalization* and is shown with a hollow arrow and a line. Taking this example further, we see that generalization can be broken down to more than two children use cases.

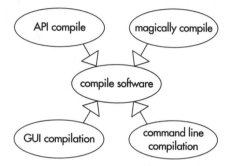

Generalization can even be hierarchical, where children use cases of a parent use case can have their own children.

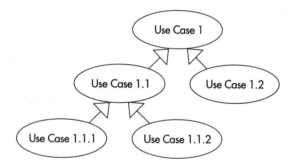

If you have generalized use cases, and an actor uses a generalized use case, you should not have that actor also use a parent of that generalized use case. In the previous example, this would mean that if your actor uses use case 1.1.1, you should not have that actor using 1.1 or 1.

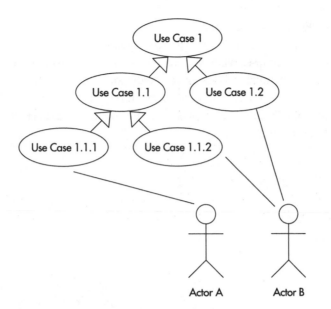

In the preceding example, if Actor B uses use cases 1.1.2 and 1.2, what would it mean if you also had that actor using use case 1?

Perhaps this is best explained with an example. In the following diagram, we use the same use case structure as the previous ones, with hierarchical generalization, and fill it in with different use cases for cooking dinner.

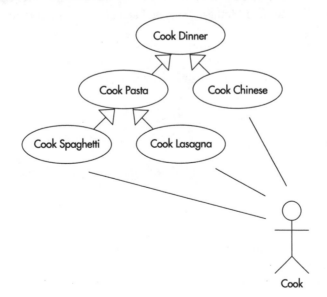

In the example, we lost one of the actors, but we will get back to this in the next section of this module. We have one actor, Cook, who will Cook Dinner by Cooking Spaghetti, Cooking Lasagna, or Cooking Chinese. What would it mean if the Cook would use Cook Pasta and Cook Lasagna? By generalizing Cook Pasta, the diagram illustrates that the child use cases, Cook Spaghetti and Cook Lasagna, inherit common functionality called Cook Pasta. It implies that the use case Cook Pasta alone is not enough, but rather it is a piece of the process that allows dinner to be cooked.

Actor to Actor Relationships

Now, let's take the thought of generalization a little further and apply it to actors. The following is the notation for generalization of actors. It is just like generalization of use cases, except we replace the two use cases with two actors.

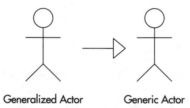

Generalized Actor   Generic Actor

This notation shows that there is a generic actor and one generalized actor that plays a more specific role in the system. If we extend our previous example of cooking dinner, we can generalize the Cook actor into Mother Cook and Father Cook, typical in most households.

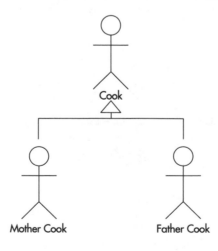

Cook

Mother Cook   Father Cook

Note that we have begun to see a different notation for generalization that is also acceptable. In this notation, we see that all generalized actors join their generalization notation of a hollow arrow into one that points to the generic actor. This can also be applied to use case generalization.

Now, taking the previous examples, we can combine our generalized actors so that they join our generalized use cases for an example of a very generalized use case diagram where Father Cook knows how to Cook Spaghetti while Mother Cook knows how to Cook Lasagna and Cook Chinese.

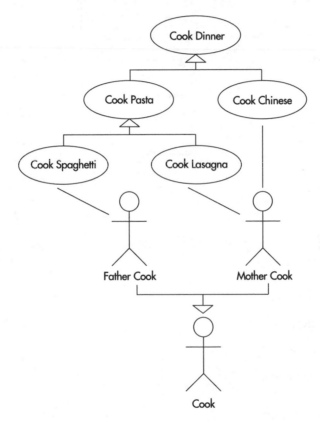

Project 2-1 Interpret the Use Case Diagram

In this project, you will interpret the following use case diagram by recognizing the UML notation that you've learned so far in this module. You will identify the actors, the use cases, and how they are related. This diagram uses the concepts of generalization that you also learned in this module.

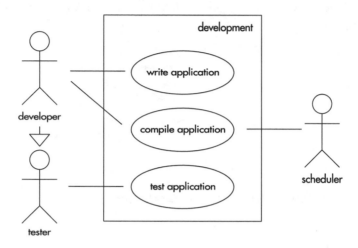

Step by Step

For this use case diagram:

1. Identify the subsystem.

2. Identify the actors.

3. Identify the use cases.

4. Identify the relationships.

Project Summary

This project gave you a chance to hone the UML notational skills that you have learned so far in this module. Before you can learn to model your own diagrams in UML, you first need to feel comfortable understanding diagrams that have already been drafted. After completing this project, you should have successfully identified three actors and three use cases. You should have also been able to identify many relationships, including a developer is a type of tester and a scheduler compiles applications.

CRITICAL SKILL
2.5 Understand How to Use Include and Extend Relationships

Including and extending are two ways of relating use cases with each other when the two are highly related to each other. The include relationship is used to indicate that a use case will include functionality from an additional use case to perform its function. Similarly, the extend relationship indicates that a use case may be extended by another use case.

Include Relationship

The following is the notation for the include relationship.

There are two types of use cases shown in this notation. The first type is called the *including* use case. This is the use case that requires functionality (include functionality) from another use case. The second type of use case is called the *included* use case. This is the use case that is included in the first, including use case. The two are connected by a dashed line and an open arrow, originating at the including use case and ending at the included use case. Finally, the word *include* is written somewhere along the arrow and encapsulated with *guillemets* (« … »).

To understand how the include relationship works, take a look at the following use case diagram that models a portion of the grading system that we started earlier in this module.

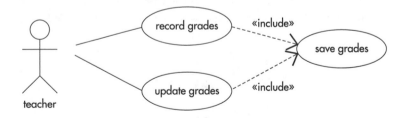

This example shows that a teacher will record grades and update grades. It also shows that both of these use cases include a common piece of functionality from a use case called Save Grades. Whenever a teacher updates grades, the grades will always be saved. Whenever a teacher records grades, the grades will always be saved.

TIP

It is very possible that you will model your include relationships as part of an iterative step in your system modeling process. As you get deeper into the modeling of your system, you will be better capable of identifying where included use cases can be used.

It is a wise idea to identify included use cases in your modeled system because it helps you identify where you can reuse functionality when you develop the system into an application. Reuse of code is one of the major benefits of component-based design and development.

Extend Relationship

Very similar to the include relationship is the extend relationship. The extend relationship notation is identical to the include relationship notation, except that the word *extend* is used within the guillemets instead of include, to indicate that one use case may be extended by another.

The use case where the dashed arrow originates is referred to as the *extending* use case, and the use case that is at the end of the dashed line, where the open arrow is pointing to, is referred to as the *extended* use case. This notation is used to identify when a use case can optionally be extended by functionality in another use case. Compared to the include relationship, where use cases must include the included use case, the extend relationship has the option of using the extended use case.

The following example will help you to understand how the extend relationship is used in context of our grading system. The Save Grades use case is extended by the Notify Guardians use case. By reading this diagram, we see that when a teacher either records or updates grades, the grades are saved and, in some cases, the guardians are notified.

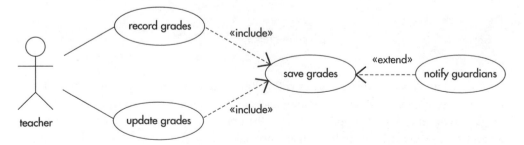

You might question why the arrow is pointing from the Notify Guardians use case to the Save Grades use case and not the other way around—after all, the guardians are notified after the grades are saved (sometimes). The reason it is drawn as shown is that the Notify Guardians use case extends the Save Grades use case. The Notify Guardians use case is functionality that is added to the Save Grades function. The Save Grades use case is not added to the Notify Guardians use case.

If the guardians were notified every time the grades where saved, the illustration would use an include relationship as shown here.

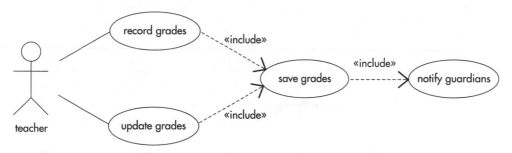

Now that you understand what an extending use case is and why it is used, you might be curious about how you are supposed to know when the guardians are notified. After all, they are notified only sometimes, and it shouldn't be random. Suppose we want to notify the guardians of a student when a failing grade is saved. We can do this using *extension points,* which allow us to indicate a condition that would allow the use case to enter into an extending use case. The following notation is used for extension points.

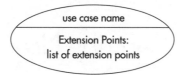

As you can see, a horizontal line divides the extended use case, and the use case name moves to the top half of the oval. Within the bottom half of the oval, the words "Extension Points:" are shown in bold with the list of possible extension points that would lead to any one of the possible extending use cases. The following is our extended use case using the extension points notation to indicate that the extending use case should be followed if a failing grade is saved.

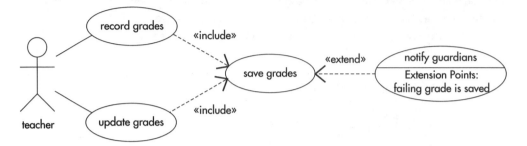

When multiple extending use cases are modeled, the extension points do not indicate which use cases extend the extended use case; they simple indicate if one is used. An extended use case can have multiple extension points and all of them must be true for a use case to be extended.

Progress Check

1. What type of relationship is used to always use another use case?

2. What type of relationship is used to occasionally use another use case?

3. What are the symbols that encapsulate the include and extend strings in the use case diagrams?

Learn How to Describe Use Cases

Use cases are described in detail using ordinary writing skills. There is really no standard for the format of use case details, although there are many techniques out there. There is no doubt that you will learn and adapt your own technique for effectively recording the details of your use cases; however, I will illustrate this task for you using the simplest form of description, a simple numbered list.

Describing use cases is the task of breaking down individual use cases into their finest details. By doing so, you will most often find that your initial list of use cases is missing some that you have now identified.

---

1. Include relationship
2. Extend relationship
3. Guillemets (« ... »)

Let's assume that we are cooking again and we want to describe the use case Cook Spaghetti. We would find the following description:

1. Put water in pot.

2. Put pot on stove.

3. Turn stove on.

4. Wait for water to boil.

5. Put spaghetti in pot.

6. Stir spaghetti occasionally.

7. When spaghetti is done, turn stove off.

8. Pour contents of pot into strainer.

Pretty basic, huh? Well what about the sauce? Do you eat plain spaghetti? After writing the description of this use case, I have remembered that we need to make sauce. It is possible that sauce will be used in the Cook Lasagna use case as well, so I would modify our use case diagram for cooking to use the include relationship so that both the Cook Spaghetti and Cook Lasagna use cases include the Make Sauce use case.

It's simple to list the activities needed to make spaghetti, but what about a use case that we will eventually be turning into software? Let's take a look at the use case for Record Grades that we introduced early in this module. When a teacher records grades, we find that the following activities need to occur:

1. The teacher identifies the student that they will be recording grades for.

2. The system looks to ensure that the student is in the database.

3. The teacher indicates for which assignment they will be entering grades.

4. The system begins a transaction in the database.

5. The system adds the assignment to the database for the student.

6. The teacher enters the grade for the student's assignment.

7. The system validates the grade entered to ensure it is within the correct range.

8. The system records the grade for the assignment.

9. The system ends the transaction.

10. The system notifies the teacher that the grade has been recorded.

This list of activities may not have been as apparent to you as was the list of activities for making spaghetti. Did you remember that a transaction needed to be created in the database? Did you remember that the grade entered by the teacher needs to be validated? The answer to these is questions most likely is no. At least you didn't know about these activities before you began writing the detailed use case descriptions for each. The wonderful thing about writing use case descriptions is that they are very easy to adapt. Remember that UML modeling is an iterative process. It is not a process of simply recording data; it is a technique and a task that needs to be done to understand what you are going to build. Take advantage of this ability when you are creating your use cases.

Notice that in the list of activities for the Record Grades use case, each activity began with either "The teacher" or "The system." This information is very important so that you can understand who has control of the application at any given time. It tells you who will respond next and what will happen. You will find that this information will help you later when you create more diagrams to extend the usefulness of your use case diagrams.

Ask the Expert

Q: **You mentioned that there are many techniques for describing use cases. Can you recommend another?**

A: It just so happens that I can. A very popular technique is to create a table with a column for each thing that will interact with your use case. In the previous example of describing the Record Grades use case, there are two things that the use case interacts with, the teacher and the system. Now, as steps, you can add rows for each activity, placing the description in the appropriate row. This is done for the Record Grades use case here:

Teacher	System
Identifies the student that they will be recording grades for	Ensures that the student is in the database
Indicates which assignment they will be entering grades for	Begins a transaction Adds the assignment to the database for the student
Enters the grade for the student's assignment	Validates the grade entered to ensure it is within the correct range Records the grade for the assignment Ends the transaction Notifies the teacher that the grade has been recorded

CRITICAL SKILL
2.7 Learn How to Model a Use Case Diagram

There are five tasks for creating use case diagrams:

1. Find the actors and use cases in the system.

2. Prioritize the use cases.

3. Detail each use case.

4. Structure the case model.

5. Prototype user interfaces.

Remember that a single person can play the role of one or more of the roles in the diagram and, in some cases, more than one person is needed to fulfill a single role. I would guess that in most cases you will be the person fulfilling just about every role in this process.

We will go over each of the preceding steps except the "prototype user interfaces" task, which is beyond the scope of this book.

Find Actors and Use Cases

The first task in creating your use case diagram is to identify the actors and use cases of the system that will be modeled. This is typically done by a system analyst who interviews potential users of your system. In some cases, this involves a face-to-face interview in which you meet with customers to ask questions and learn about what they need. During this interview, you can either create a written transcript or simply take a lot of notes to use later. In other cases, somebody in your company will provide you with a list of business requirements for the project. From these business requirements, you need to ask the provider questions to find the answers you need. These requirements and the answers you receive to your questions will become the notes you use to create your use case diagrams.

The following is a list of business requirements that have been provided for us to help create our use cases:

● We need a system with which teachers can record grades for students.

● The system needs to generate report cards on command.

● The system needs to allow users to view the grades that are recorded.

Not much information to build a product with, is there? Well, now it is our job to find out more information about the requests. Usually, all the information that you require to work on the project is not realized by the people who are giving you the information. A good tracking system and management process is needed at this time so that changes to requirements after this point are minimized and so that you do not work for requirements that were never "officially" approved. I'll leave you to worry about how to handle this at your company. I recommend *Code Complete* by Steve C. McConnell (Microsoft Press, 1993) as an excellent source of information regarding software development process management.

Now we need to ask the provider of our business requirements for more information about what they want. In this case, product management (PM) has provided us with the business requirements previously listed. The following is a list of questions that we have asked product management and their responses:

Question: Can teachers update grades that have already been entered?

Answer: Of course!

Question: Who creates the report cards, the teachers?

Answer: No…we have an administrative person who does that.

Question: Once the report cards are created, do we do anything with them?

Answer: After they are created, we should check them for accuracy—our administrative person can do this. When they are approved, the teachers should distribute them electronically.

Question: Who will need to view the grades?

Answer: The teachers and the students.

That taught us a lot. After this interview, we should find that we have a new list of updated requirements for the system:

- We need a system with which teachers can record and update grades for students.
- The system needs to generate report cards on command by an administrator, who will check them for accuracy.
- The teachers will distribute the report cards electronically.
- The system needs to allow teachers and students to view the grades that are recorded.

From our revised business requirements, we should be able to come up with an adequate list of actors by finding the people or things that interact with the system. We ask the question "Who or what will use this system?" In response, we identify our actors as the teachers, students, and administrator.

Next, we must identify the use cases that our actors will use to get the system to function. This can be done by asking the question "What will the system do?" In response, we come up with the following use cases:

● Record Grades

● Update Grades

● Generate Report Cards

● Check Report Cards for Accuracy

● Distribute Report Cards

● View Grades

As we move through the steps of creating our use case diagrams, we will find that we will identify new use cases as we get into more detail. We will also find that some that we thought were needed are not needed.

Prioritize Use Cases

The next step in creating use case diagrams is to prioritize the use cases that we have identified so far. This task is usually done by the architect of the system who would have the best overall idea of what tasks are the most crucial and which ones are the hardest to work on. They would also identify which use cases can provide reuse for other use cases, thus saving time in the long run. The skills involved for prioritizing use cases come with experience and are beyond the scope of this book. However, with our limited list of requirements, we can easily come up with the following priority list:

1. Record grades.

2. View grades.

3. Update grades.

4. Generate report cards.

5. Check report cards for accuracy.

6. Distribute report cards.

Some use cases have to come before others because they are dependent upon each other. For instance, you cannot do anything until the system has grades in it, so Record Grades is obviously the most important use case.

Detail Each Use Case

For each use case that we have, the use-case specifier role needs to create detailed descriptions so that we fully understand the tasks that are involved in creating our system. It would not be unusual for the use-case specifier role to interact with the system analyst and the people who were originally interviewed for the business requirements in order to hash out the details of each use case more fully. After possibly one or more iterations of the interview with the appropriate people, you can continue to describe each of the use cases in detail. The following is the list of details that we have created for the use case Record Grades:

1. The teacher identifies the student that they will be recording grades for.

2. The system looks to ensure that the student is in the database.

3. The teacher indicates for which assignment they will be entering grades.

4. The system begins a transaction in the database.

5. The system adds the assignment to the database for the student.

6. The teacher enters the grade for the student's assignment.

7. The system validates the grade entered to ensure it is within the correct range.

8. The system records the grade for the assignment.

9. The system ends the transaction.

10. The system notifies the teacher that the grade has been recorded.

For the View Grades use case, we find that we need a way for somebody to log on to the system, which we immediately see will be a common use case that should be included by every other use case. Therefore, we add the Logon use case.

For the Update Grades use case, we immediately see that the Load Grades and Save Grades use cases are shared with the Record Grades and View Grades use cases and that they should both be added to our list (and therefore also described in detail).

We find that the Generate Report Cards use case is fairly straightforward. We will use the Logon use case that we have identified earlier.

When we get to the Check Report Cards for Accuracy use case, we realize that this is a manual process, not one that we can program, so we can remove it from our list of use cases. We do see that the administrator will need to view the grades to manually check them, but we already have the View Grades use case in our list, so we are safe.

Finally, we find nothing unusual about the Distribute Report Cards use case when we describe it in detail, so we make no changes.

When we have finished describing all the previously existing use cases and all the newly found use cases, we should have detailed descriptions of the following use cases:

- Logon

- Save Grades

- Record Grades

- Load Grades

- View Grades

- Update Grades

- Generate Report Cards

- Distribute Report Cards

We have added the new use cases to our list and have placed them according to their priority, which means that each new use case needs to be created before any use cases that use it.

Structure the Use Case Model

The system analyst is now called upon again to put the actors and use cases that have been identified and detailed into a use case diagram. At this point, the system analyst will leverage their knowledge of relationships (include and extend) and generalization to give the case model the appropriate structure. For our example that we've been working on throughout this module, the following illustration is the result of our hard work:

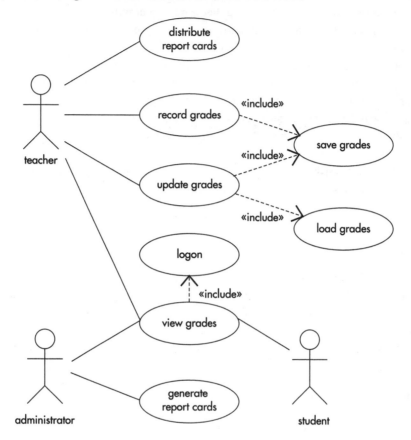

Remember that the entire Unified Process is an iterative process. Nobody expects you to pull the preceding diagram out of your hat the first round of modeling. This entire module has built upon the concepts of use case diagram UML notation, and we have gone through the iterative process to produce the preceding result.

Let's read through the diagram together:

- A teacher can record grades. Recording grades includes saving grades.

- A teacher can update grades. Updating grades includes loading and saving grades.

- A teacher, an administrator, and a student can view grades, which includes logging in.

- An administrator can generate report cards.

- A teacher can distribute report cards.

Project 2-2 Model a Use Case Diagram

In this project, you will take the following business requirements and create a use case diagram for them. You will leverage your knowledge of UML notation for use case diagrams, including actors, use cases, the different types of relationships, and generalization. You will pick one use case and detail it using the numbered list method.

The following requirements are for a point-of-sale product:

- The system will allow the administrator to run inventory reports by loading inventory data from disk.

- The administrator can update the inventory by loading and saving the inventory data to and from a disk.

- A sales clerk records walk-in sales.

- A telephone operator is a special type of sales clerk who handles phone orders.

- Any kind of sale must update the inventory.

- A sale may need to verify a credit card if the purchase is a credit card purchase.

- A sale may need to verify a check if the purchase is a check purchase.

Step by Step

1. Identify the actors of your system.

2. Identify the use cases of your system.

3. Prioritize your use cases.

4. Detail each use case in the order that it is prioritized.

5. Identify the generalizations in each use case.

(continued)

TIP

Whenever you can say that "Item A is a type of Item B," you have found
a generalization.

6. Identify the include relationships in each use case.

TIP

Remember that include relationships are identified when one use case always
uses another use case.

7. Identify the extend relationships in each use case.

TIP

Remember that extend relationships are identified when one use case may use another
use case.

8. Create a use case diagram for each use case with the actors, use cases, generalizations,
include relationships, and extend relationships that you have identified.

Project Summary

In this project, you should have successfully created use case diagrams from only the
requirements supplied to you. The next illustration is an example of a use case diagram
that you may have created for an Update Inventory use case.

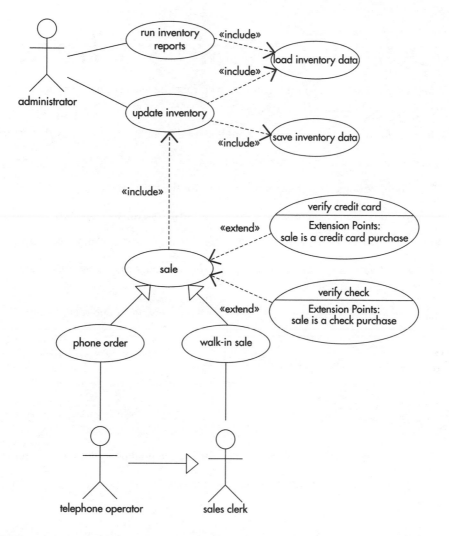

With your use case diagram, you will continue to model your system in more detail in the next modules, but first you are going to learn about object-oriented design and analysis in Module 3, specifically how it applies to UML and the Unified Process.

✓ Module 2 Mastery Check

1. What is a good actor name for the person who runs the weekly payroll checks on a payroll system?

2. What would be some use cases that would be used in a payroll system by this actor?

3. Model a use case diagram for the paycheck system.

4. What would be some generalization use cases for the use case Send Letter?

5. What would be some generalization actors for the actor Army Personnel?

6. What is the difference between an include relationship and an extend relationship?

7. What would be a valid included use case for the including cases Print Document, Print Envelope, and Print Label?

8. List the extension points that can be used for the following extend relationship.

9. Describe the use case Save Grades as it applied to the grading system used in this module.

10. What are the steps used to create a use case diagram?

Module 3

Introduction to Object-Oriented Design

I know you've heard the term "object-oriented" before, but do you really know what it means? If you aren't familiar with object-oriented design, analysis, or programming, you are probably familiar with procedural design. *Procedural design* describes the techniques that are used to write an application that has multiple procedures that modify *global* data.

Object-oriented design, on the other hand, describes the techniques that are used to write an application in which objects with their own data and functionality use that data to talk to other objects in order to complete a task.

We are discussing object-oriented design in this book because UML is used to model object-oriented application structures.

CRITICAL SKILL
3.1
Identify the Characteristics of Object-Oriented Design

Object-oriented design is the technique used to architect software with groups of classes that interact with one another to solve a problem. A class is a representation of a generalized thing, such as an animal, a person, a car, a ticket, or a system.

A class exposes itself through an interface, which is a collection of attributes and operations that allow other classes to interact with it. A person may have attributes such as their name, hair color, eye color, height, weight, sex, and age. A class has methods that are exposed to other classes so that they can tell a class what to do. For instance, a person might have the methods walk, sit, stand, sleep, and talk.

An object is an instance of a class with its own set of data, giving it a class with state. If we have a ticket class, then a ticket for seat 4a to Lenny Kravitz playing the Beacon Theater on Halloween would be an object, because it has definite state through its own set of data.

To qualify as an object-oriented design, a few requirements need to be met. The following three principles are essential for an object-oriented design to exist:

● Classes (abstraction and encapsulation)

● Inheritance

● Polymorphism

With these principles, object-oriented design allows us to design complex systems by constructing them out of simple, smaller pieces that interact with each other. The rest of this module will discuss each of these principles in detail.

Ask the Expert

Q: What is the difference between object-oriented analysis (OOA), object-oriented design (OOD), and object-oriented programming (OOP)?

A: Object-oriented *analysis* is the process that is used to attempt to understand (analyze) a system using classes and objects for the world relating to the system. It is the process of creating a vocabulary to describe the system that is to be modeled.

Object-oriented *design* is the method used to record the vocabulary found in the analysis phase. It gives the model behavior that is required for the system to exist.

Object-oriented *programming* is the actual implementation of the model created in the object-oriented design.

The normal progression, or waterfall method, is from OOA to OOD and then to OOP (analysis, design, and programming). Alternative methods have been designed, such as the spiral and iterative methods. The spiral method adds prototyping and risk management to each stage. The first stage is OOA, prototyping, and risk management. The second stage is OOD, prototyping, and risk management. The third stage is OOP, prototyping, and risk management. The iterative method consists of doing a little of each stage, repeatedly. Do a little OOA, then a little OOD, and then a little OOP, and then start over.

Most projects actually fall into a combination of these three techniques—but they all consist of some sort of analysis, design, and programming.

CRITICAL SKILL
3.2 Understand the Use of Classes in OOD

You will be learning how to model classes in later modules of this book, but for now, let's take a moment to discuss what really makes a class a class. There are basically two things that do this: abstraction and encapsulation. *Abstraction* is the method of creating general terms for an item, while *encapsulation* is the method of stuffing that item with the functionality and data that pertain to it. Encapsulation is the characteristic of object-oriented design that says that how a class operates is nobody's business but its own. It means that all of the specifics about how it does things are encapsulated within itself. On top of this, interfaces are used within classes to separate the functionality from the means to invoke it. We'll get to more details about encapsulation and interfaces shortly. Let us first take a deeper look at abstraction.

Abstraction

Abstraction is probably the most common characteristic of anything that is object-oriented. To be abstract is defined by *The American Heritage Dictionary,* 4th ed. (www.dictionary.com) as "Thought of or stated without reference to a specific instance." An object is an abstraction. It is a generalized form of something without a specific type.

One of the most common examples of abstraction in object-oriented design is the automobile. An automobile would be a class that is very generalized because it has properties and functionality that are common to all automobiles regardless of whether they are cars, trucks, sport utility vehicles, or buses. For instance, an automobile has wheels, seats, a steering wheel, an engine, lights, and doors. Each type of automobile may have different types or numbers of these properties, but they all have them. For instance, a truck may have 18 wheels while a car typically has 4 wheels.

Every automobile drives, parks, and goes in reverse. How each automobile does this depends on its individual design. For instance, a truck may use diesel fuel to move while a car usually uses unleaded gasoline. An SUV and a truck probably go into four-wheel drive at times, but a bus does not. All automobiles still drive, thus abstracting the functionality of all specific automobile types.

TIP

An easy way to identify a class for something is to put it into this phrase:
"A _____ is a type of _____." For example:
A car is a type of automobile.
A truck is a type of automobile.
A bus is a type of automobile.

Although automobile is a class, it can be abstracted even more:
An automobile is a type of transportation.
A plane is a type of transportation.
A ship is a type of transportation.

Progress Check

1. What is the difference between procedural and object-oriented design?

2. What are the three major principles of object-oriented design?

3. What is data abstraction?

Encapsulation

Encapsulation is the characteristic of object-oriented design that says that an object shall operate as a black box. *Black box* is a term used for something that has known functionality but the means in which this functionality is carried out is unknown. The functionality of an object is hidden, with encapsulation, from all other objects.

Other objects that interact with a particular black box object do not know what the black box is doing internally. They do not know what data is in the black box, other than the data they give it. They do not know what the black box is doing to the data. They only know what they give to the black box, what they ask the black box to do, and what the black box gives back to them.

---

1. Procedural design entails every function accessing one another without boundaries. Object-oriented design is the separation of data and functionality into common classes that interact with each other to create a system.

2. Classes, inheritance, and polymorphism

3. The generalizing of an item without a type

In more specific terms, this means that the interface of an object is separate from the implementation of an object. Expanding on the previous example of the abstract automobile object, as a black box, the automobile does not let other automobiles know how much gas it has, what its temperature is, or how it is using the unleaded gasoline to make itself move. It does accept gasoline and it does move, but all the steps and factors in between are hidden, or encapsulated.

Interfaces

By hiding functionality from the user in this way, we improve our software, because it becomes easier to use and easier to read. These two benefits ultimately mean that encapsulation helps lower maintenance and prevent problems.

As any program grows in size, so does the chance that you, as the developer, will lose grasp of the reins that control it. It is not uncommon for large applications to be hundreds of thousands of lines of code. I have worked on a couple of projects with close to 500,000 lines of code in each.

With a procedural design without encapsulation, everything is exposed. Pieces of functionality begin to interfere with one another very easily, because there are no interfaces defined. Business rules (important business logic) sometimes get bypassed because the procedures that implement them do not need to be called. Simply updating business rules does not always update the entire application, because they can be bypassed. This is where we get the term "spaghetti code"; the lines of operation are tangled because any piece of functionality can call any other piece of functionality.

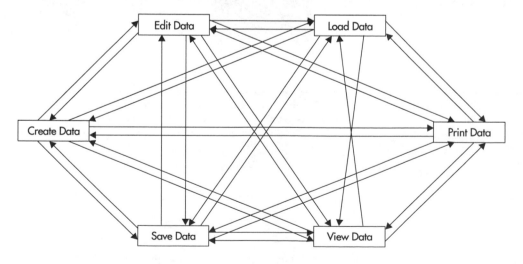

However, with object-oriented development, the use of encapsulation and exposure through interfaces helps maintain coherence in your software. With encapsulation, you can create objects to store data, objects to display data, and objects that carry out business logic on your data.

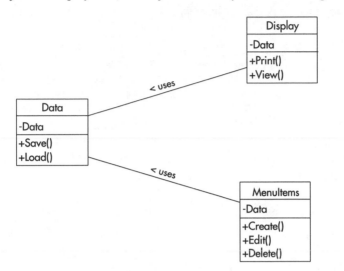

Progress Check

1. What is encapsulation?

2. What is a black box?

3. What is an interface?

CRITICAL SKILL
3.3 Understand the Use of Inheritance in OOD

Inheritance is a way of allowing one class to gain (inherit) the functionality of another class. By doing this we can write code once and reuse it throughout our application. This gives us the

---

1. The hiding of internal functionality from others
2. Something that produces an output from an input, without exposing how it is done
3. Exposed functionality

advantage of having smaller, cleaner code. You only need to change a piece of functionality in one place to fix the entire application. Inheritance allows your system to have a class that does everything another class does plus more.

Assume for a moment, that we have two classes, Lion and Bird, with similar functionality.

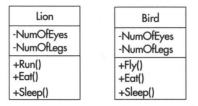

These classes have a common functionality that can be shared between the two. In UML, we can use the generalization notation to illustrate this.

As you can see, two notations actually exist—one with a single, shared open arrow, and the other with separate open arrows. The classes where the arrows originate are called *subclasses*, or *derived classes*. The class where the arrows terminate is called the *superclass*, or the *base class*. In the notation shown in the preceding illustration, we would say that SubclassA is derived from Superclass.

Now, if we were to remodel our Lion and Bird classes to utilize inheritance shown with class generalization, we would need to come up with a name of a class that would contain the common functionality. This class would need to be a more general form of each class. Considering that both a lion and a bird are types of animals, we would most likely create an Animal class to contain the common functionality.

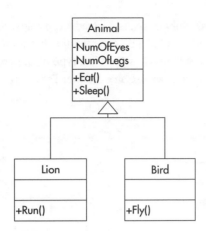

This illustration shows that the Bird and Lion classes are each derived from Animal. The Animal class now contains the common functionality to the two subclasses (this includes the attributes NumOfEyes and NumOfLegs as well as the operations Eat and Sleep). Because a lion can't fly, the Bird class will own that method instead of giving it up to the superclass, Animal. Similarly, the Lion class has an operation, Run, which a bird cannot do.

We definitely made inheritance seem easy in this section, but believe me, it isn't. As you will soon see, things like inheritance hierarchies (inheritance that spans multiple levels) and multiple inheritance (a class that inherits functionality from more than one other class) begin to complicate the entire situation. It takes a lot of practice, a solid understanding, and a quiet cubicle to fully understand many of these theories, but I can guarantee that, one day, if you work with this enough, it will become second nature, as is true for many things in software development.

Inheritance Hierarchies

Inheritance can span multiple levels. A superclass to a subclass can also be a subclass to another superclass.

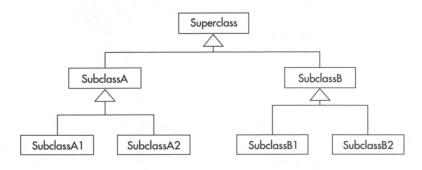

In this diagram, the class, SubclassA, is derived from Superclass, but it is also the base class for SubclassA1 and SubclassA2. You can read this hierarchy as follows: SubclassA1 and SubclassA2 are types of SubclassA, which is a type of Superclass.

This might make more sense if we use an example. Take a look at the automobile example:

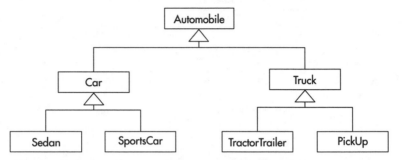

In this example, a Car class and a Truck class are both types of the Automobile class, but it doesn't stop there. We also see that a Sedan class and a SportsCar class are both types of the Car class, and a TractorTrailer class and a PickUp class are both types of the Truck class. We can break classes into this structure to give each its own distinct functionality, or its own distinct ways of performing its functionality. If we wanted to take our automobile example another step forward, we could give each class appropriate attributes and operations.

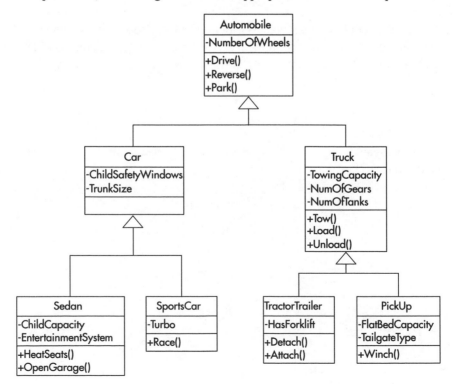

Now this is starting to get really interesting. You can see how easy it is to break the functionality into the proper category or class. The SportsCar class has a Race operation because sports cars are the only type of automobile that can race, but both sedans and sports cars have trunks, and therefore the more general Car class contains the TrunkSize attribute.

Multiple Inheritance

Just as you thought it couldn't get any more involved, you learn that classes can be derived from more than one superclass. As an example, think of a tank—it can be a type of vehicle and it can be a type of weapon.

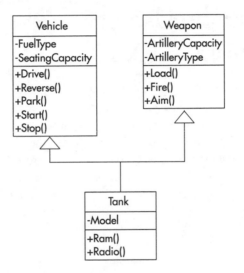

This notation might have been what you would have expected, one subclass with open arrows pointing to two superclasses. This illustration identifies that the functionality of moving belongs to the Vehicle class through its operations Drive, Reverse, Park, Start, and Stop, while the functionality to destroy belongs to the Weapon class through its Load, Aim, and Fire operations. The operations Ram and Radio are only found in the Tank class.

Progress Check

1. What is inheritance?

2. What is another name for a derived class? What about a base class?

3. What is the difference between hierarchical inheritance and multiple inheritance?

CRITICAL SKILL
3.4 Understand the Use of Polymorphism in OOD

Polymorphism is the final principle of object-oriented design. It is the ability of two or more abstract classes to have the same interface, but to operate on their data differently because each has its own set of code, or way of doing something. For instance, recall our previous example of the Lion and Bird classes. Our original model indicated that the Sleep operation belonged to the Animal class, meaning that the functionality to sleep was controlled by the base class, Animal.

If we wanted to model that each class, Lion and Bird, slept differently (one sleeps lying down, the other sleeps standing up), we would add the operation to the individual classes.

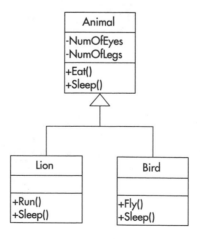

---

1. The gaining (inheriting) of functionality from a parent class

2. Subclass; superclass

3. Hierarchical inheritance is when a class is both a subclass and a superclass in the same model, whereas multiple inheritance is when a single class can have more than one superclass.

Project 3-1   Creating a Class Diagram

In this project, you will create a class diagram using notation that you haven't quite learned yet. The notation is not as important at this time as are the concepts. The following facts give you the information you need to construct a class diagram:

- A student can be an undergraduate or a graduate student.

- An undergraduate student can be a type of tutor.

- A tutor tutors a student.

- A teacher and a professor are two types of instructors.

- A teacher assistant can assist a teacher and a professor, but a teacher can be assisted by only one assistant, while a professor can be assisted by up to five assistants.

- A teacher assistant is a type of graduate student.

Step by Step

1. Model "A student can be an undergraduate or a graduate student" as three classes, Student, UnderGraduate, and Graduate. The UnderGraduate and Graduate classes should be subclasses of the Student class.

NOTE

Since we have not yet discussed how to model class diagrams, the answers for each step are included *for this project only*. The purpose of this module is to explain object-oriented techniques, not to show you how to model class diagrams.

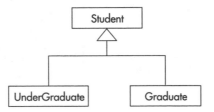

(continued)

2. Model "An undergraduate student can be a type of tutor" by creating a new class, Tutor, which is the second base class to the UnderGraduate class.

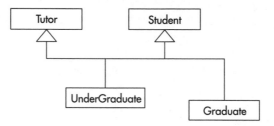

3. Model "A tutor tutors a student" by creating an association from the Tutor class to the Student class with the association name of "tutors >."

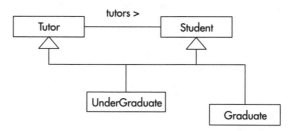

4. Model "A teacher and a professor are two types of instructors" as three classes, Instructor, Teacher, and Professor. The Professor and Teacher classes should be subclasses of the Instructor class.

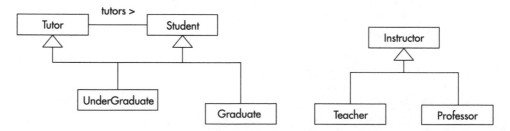

5. Model "A teacher assistant can assist a teacher and a professor, but a teacher can be assisted by only one assistant, while a professor can be assisted by up to four assistants." Create another class called TeacherAssistant, relating to both the Teacher and the Professor classes, with the association name as "assists >" in both cases. You can set the multiplicity on each of the associations, at both ends. For the Teacher – TeacherAssistant association, the multiplicity is 1 Teacher can be assisted by 0..1 TeacherAssistants. The Professor – TeacherAssistant association's multiplicity can be read as 1 Professor can be assisted by 0..4 TeacherAssistants.

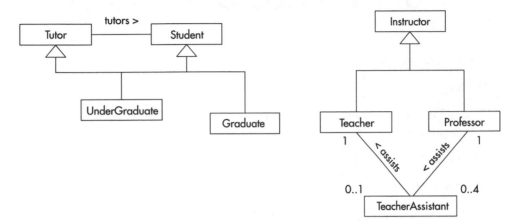

6. Model "A teacher assistant is a type of graduate student" and tie the two separate models together by making the TeacherAssistant class a derived class of the Graduate base class.

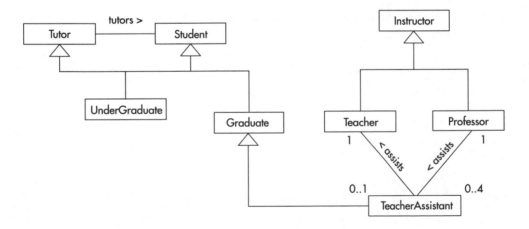

Project Summary

In this module, you learned that object-oriented design requires abstraction, encapsulation, inheritance, and polymorphism. Although we haven't touched upon the UML notation for class diagrams yet, you have modeled multiple inheritance and inheritance hierarchies. Don't worry, there is still plenty more notation to learn, but we won't get to that until Module 6. The next module will show you how to model business objects as you enter the first step of the second phase of the Unified Process, elaboration.

Module 3 Mastery Check

1. What is abstraction?

2. What is encapsulation?

3. What is inheritance?

4. Diagram the generalization of a file. Include three types of files and label the subclasses and superclass.

5. What is multiple inheritance?

6. What is hierarchical inheritance?

7. Start with a superclass, Computer Accessory, and diagram three levels of subclasses.

8. What is polymorphism?

9. How does object-oriented design help code reuse?

10. What are some common functionality or attributes belonging to a hard drive, floppy drive, and CD-ROM drive?

Module 4

Workflow Modeling with Activity Diagrams

CRITICAL SKILLS

This module introduces you to activity diagrams, which are used to model flow between different components of an object-oriented system. With activity diagrams, you will be able to illustrate where functionality exists in your system and how the functionality, coordinated with functionality of other pieces of your system, will be used to meet the business requirements that you modeled earlier using use case diagrams.

CRITICAL SKILL
4.1 # Define Activity Diagrams

Activity diagrams provide much needed descriptions of a system by providing the next step in analyzing the system, following the use case diagrams. An activity diagram allows the reader to see the system's execution and how it changes direction based upon different conditions and stimuli. In this way, activity diagrams are used to model workflows for use cases. Although activity diagrams can also be used to model complex object behavior when you get into the system design portion of your modeling, this module deals primarily with the analysis phase using the activity diagrams as a means for taking your use cases to the next level.

CRITICAL SKILL
4.2 # Discover Why We Model Activity Diagrams

Activity diagrams are helpful, particularly to use cases, because they give the reader an obvious start and end state. When used to model the workflows of a use case, activity diagrams can show the paths within the use case as well as between use cases.

Activity diagrams can explain to the reader what conditions need to be met for a use case to be valid, as well as the conditions, or states, a system is left in once the use case has completed.

Because we know that the Unified Process is an iterative process, when we are modeling activity diagrams, we often find ourselves discovering additional use cases that we hadn't thought of earlier. In some cases, we discover common functionality that can be separated into its own use case. This ultimately saves us time when we develop the application.

Progress Check

1. What are the two major roles of an activity diagram?

2. What are three reasons why we model activity diagrams?

---

1. To model use case and complex object workflows
2. To elaborate on a use case, to identify the pre- and postconditions of a use case, and to discover new use cases

CRITICAL SKILL
4.3 Identify the Notational Components
of Activity Diagrams

An activity diagram reminds many of the traditional flow diagram, except that the notation is slightly different.

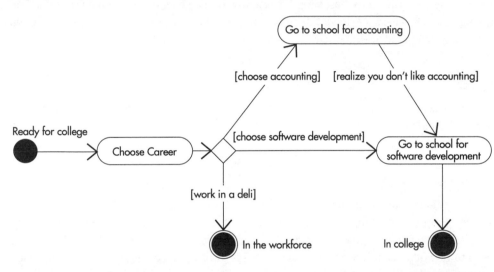

There are three major notational components to activity diagrams: activities, states, and transitions. Everything else that you learn in this module will be an enhancement to any one of these components.

An activity is also called an *action state.* It is an indicator within the diagram that something is to be done. In the previous example, Choose Career is the first activity shown. States are an indication of internal values. A state may indicate whether a field is dirty, or it may indicate success or failure. When a state is modeled in an activity diagram, it is used because it has importance. It may be used to indicate that the system is behaving differently or that it has met a set of criteria. To combine activities and states, transitions show the migration paths around the activity diagram.

Activities: Action States

The notation for an activity is a rectangle with very rounded corners ("very rounded" relative to the notation for states, discussed next, which is very similar but with less rounded corners).

You may even think of an activity as a circle that has been cut in half and elongated in the middle, like a stretch limousine.

Name of Action

Activities indicate action, and therefore should be named appropriately. When deciding on the names of your activities, choose a few words that accurately describe the action that is taking place. For instance, Save File or Create New Document would be descriptive activity names, as compared to Run or Update, which appear to the reader to be incomplete.

States

A state is drawn similarly to an activity, except, as previously mentioned, the corners of a state are less rounded.

Name of State

States are usually identified with a word or a phrase that indicates the current being of a system. For example, Stopped would be a state, whereas Stop would be used as an activity.

States can communicate milestones in an activity diagram for the reader or they can be used to flag other conditions later in the workflow. For instance, the states of the use case called Drive Car may be Parked, Idle, First Gear, Second Gear, Third Gear, Fourth Gear, and Reverse.

UML describes two special states, the start and end states. A start state is indicated as a solid-black dot, while the end state is drawn as a black dot with a circle around it.

● Start State   ◉ End State

Each activity diagram can have only one start state, but it can have countless end states. Just remember that modeling is supposed to make your life as an analyst and designer easier—not harder. I would avoid using too many end states for this reason.

◉ Grades Recorded

● Ready to record grades   ◉ User Error

◉ Operation Cancelled

As you can see from the preceding example, you can label each start and end state as you would ordinary states.

Progress Check

1. What are the three major notational components of an activity diagram?

2. What is the difference between an activity and a state?

3. What are the two special states?

Transitions

Transitions are used to show control flow from one state to another. They can show flow from a state to an activity, between activities, or between states. The notation for a transition is an open arrow pointing in the direction of the control flow.

---

1. Activities, states, and transitions.

2. An activity indicates that an action is taking place, whereas a state indicates that a milestone or internal setting has changed.

3. Start state and end state.

Putting it Together

Now that we have seen all three of the notational components of the activity diagram, we can put them together to form our first activity diagram.

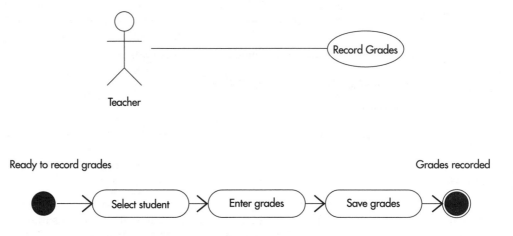

In this example, we prove that there is more information for a use case than what is modeled in the use case diagram. Starting with a use case that shows that a Teacher records grades, we have created an activity diagram that shows the three steps necessary for the teacher to record grades (select student, enter grades, and save grades).

**CRITICAL SKILL
4.4** Learn How to Use Conditions

Conditions are necessary additions to transitions to change the direction of any workflow. Without any conditions, everything would start at point A and continue to point B without any chance of deviation. Because we are modeling workflows here, lack of deviation rarely helps us, so we will learn how to use conditions to enhance our diagrams.

With the use of guards and decision points, we can model conditions that alter the flow of our diagram. Guards are used to allow the control to flow only in a direction that meets a prerequisite, whereas decision points require a decision to determine in which direction the flow will continue.

Guards

A guard is noted on a transition between two activities or states, and is enclosed in brackets (for example, [guardname]).

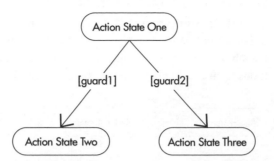

In the preceding example, control flow will go from Action State One to Action State Two if [guard1] is True, but it will flow from Action State One to Action State Three if [guard2] is True. In the following example, when the user saves a file, guards are used to determine how to save the file. If the file already exists, then it is updated; if the file does not exist, a new one is created.

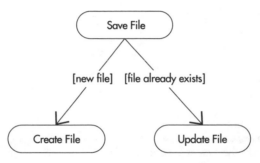

Decision Points

Decision points, for all practical purposes, do the same thing as ordinary guards do, but they do it more neatly, especially if you have a large diagram with a lot of different conditions. By using the notation of a diamond, from which all the conditional guards branch, the transitions are kept from the originating activity and moved to a focal point where the activity transitions to. This gives the appearance to the reader that the action completes by making a decision.

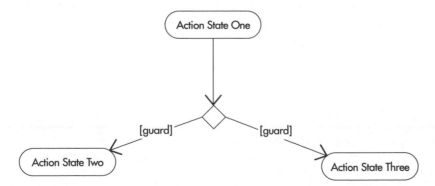

You'll notice that guards are still used with decision points, but from the transitions branching from the decision point rather than from the calling activity. When laying out your activity diagram for readability, the decision point adds to the convenience because it spaces the conditional transitions from each other, giving it some space to itself.

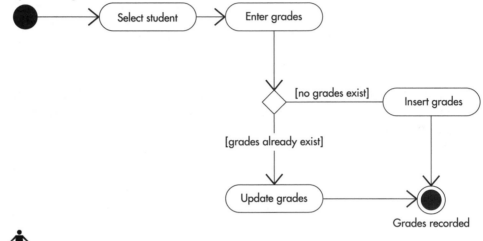

TIP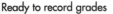

As you get into more and more complex UML diagramming, you may find it useful to draw outlines of the model on paper to see how to best place the activities, decision points, and states. You don't have to fill them all in; instead, simply draw a small (two-inch square) diagram with directions for where the activity and state shapes and the diamonds go, and then draw the lines and arrows. If everything fits right, you can take the time to redraw it on a clean sheet of paper. Even when using a case tool such as Visio, I find that this technique saves more time than dragging and dropping controls on the screen to view different layout styles.

Progress Check

1. What is a transition?

2. What are decision points?

3. What are guards?

1. A representation of control flow from one activity or state to another
2. Notation to indicate that a decision will be made and control can flow to different locations accordingly
3. Expressions that, when evaluated to True, allow control to flow across their transitions

Project 4-1   Reading an Activity Diagram

In this project, you will read the following activity diagram, which depicts how to decide on what to eat. While reading the diagram, identify all the notational components that you have learned so far in this module.

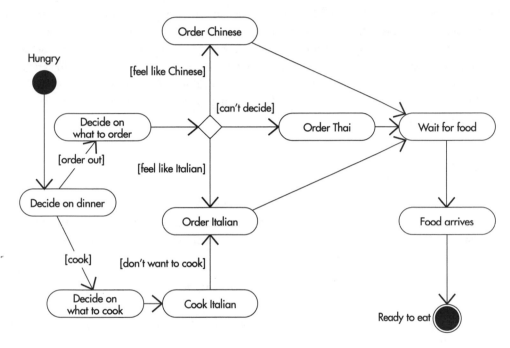

Step by Step

1. Identify the conditional areas of the activity diagram.

2. Identify the start and stop states in the activity diagram.

3. Identify the control flows in the activity diagram.

Project Summary

This project has proven that you can read an activity diagram from the start state to the stop states. You should have been able to identify the conditional cases of the activity diagram including: when the activity Cook Italian has completed, the flow will go to Order Italian if the guard [don't want to cook] is True; otherwise, the flow will not progress. In addition, you should have been able to identify the start and stop conditions, as well as the control flows modeled in the activity diagram.

Understand Other Notations Available in Activity Diagrams

In addition to the basics that you have learned thus far with activity diagrams, there are several more notational extras that you can use to enhance your diagramming techniques. The use of *events* and *triggers* is similar to the use of guards, except instead of controlling flow by restricting based upon an expression, events and triggers are fired to move the control flow in the respective direction. *Swim lanes* are used to isolate activities according to their domain, or object. And, finally, *forks* and *joins* are used for parallel processing of transitions (when two transitions can occur at the same time).

Events and Triggers

Events are very similar to operations or methods (as you may be familiar with from your programming experience). Events are a higher-level analysis-notational component (we're still in the analysis phase) than are their design counterparts, the operations. Events are indicators that an action has taken place. They can contain one or more arguments, located within parentheses following the event name.

Eventname (arguments)

Events can be included on transitions to indicate that processing is forcing control to move in a particular direction.

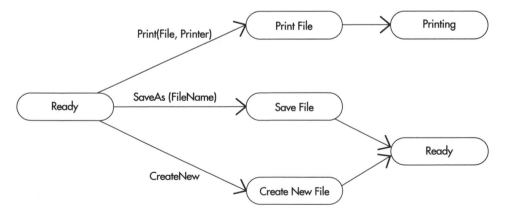

In the preceding example, the control flow can go in one of three directions based upon the event that triggers the flow to leave the Ready state and to move to a corresponding activity. The first event, Print, takes two arguments, the file and the printer, to the Print File activity. The second event, SaveAs, simply takes a filename to the Save File activity. The final event, CreateNew, doesn't need any arguments, because it brings the control flow to the Create New File activity.

Swimming

Swim lanes are neat because they really enhance the readability of an activity diagram to a large degree. Simply notated as large rectangular boxes with the name of the object or domain at the top of them, swim lanes are used to contain activities to their corresponding home.

Lane One	Lane Two	Lane Three

The following example shows an activity diagram as it progresses back and forth between the Teacher and the Web Interface, crisscrossing control flow. Without the swim lanes, this activity diagram could not tell you that the Teacher uses the Logon, Choose Student, and

Change Student Info activities and the Web Interface uses the Validate User, Retrieve Student Info, and Persist User Info activities.

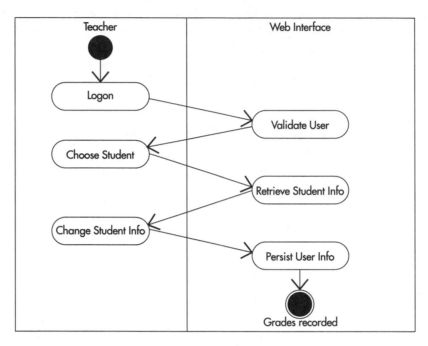

Although you might be able to infer which object or domain an activity belongs to while reading these examples, as you get more experienced with UML, you will find that the diagrams become more and more difficult. Of course, your ability will grow as well, but the ability to read the modeler's mind doesn't. The swim lanes are a great way to get your point across in any activity diagram, and I highly recommend using them any time your model involves more than one object.

Forks and Joins

Forks allow parallel processes to begin, and joins allow parallel processes to catch up and resume a single-process flow. When a fork is encountered within an activity diagram, each branch of the fork is, in essence, its own separate activity diagram, with no respect for any of the others. Each of the control flows doesn't have to wait for the other—that is, until one comes to a join.

Both forks and joins are represented similarly within UML. They both have a thick-black line. Forks have one transition entering and two or more exiting. This depicts the single-process control flow splitting into multiple control flows. Joins, on the other hand, have the exact opposite. They have two or more transitions entering the join and only one exiting. This depicts the distinct processes coming together to reform a single process.

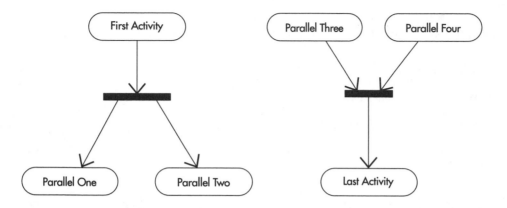

If one process arrives at a join before the other, it waits and control never passes the join until both processes are ready.

The following example illustrates how one process following a fork may take longer than another. Of course, this is completely assumed by the number of activities in each process. Because we don't know how long each activity takes, we cannot guarantee which one will complete first. Because of this, we have a join right before we give the user access to the application, to ensure that the two separate processes catch up with each other.

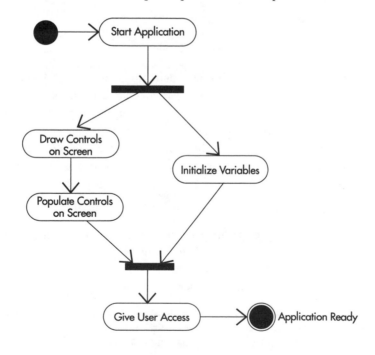

Progress Check

1. What are events?

2. What are swim lanes used for?

3. What are forks and joins used for?

Learn How to Model an Activity Diagram

There are five tasks for creating activity diagrams:

1. Identify the use cases that require activity diagrams.

2. Model primary paths for each use case.

3. Model alternative paths for each use case.

4. Add swim lanes for identifying business areas for activities.

5. Refine high-level activities into more activity diagrams.

As we go through each step, we will slowly build upon our activity diagram. As you recall, the Unified Process is an iterative one. Never be ashamed to come back to an earlier stage to clarify a model or a portion of a model. As you do this, you should see how your changes affect the whole project, by reviewing the models that come after the one you have changed. These changes, made early, are what modeling software is all about. You benefit from making your mistakes early in the process; better stated, you benefit from hashing out your ideas early.

Identifying Use Cases

Before we can begin modeling an activity diagram, we have to decide on what to model. We will start from a use case from Module 2. The following use case, in which a teacher updates grades, was part of a much larger set of use cases, but we will start here. A system will require that you use many, many diagrams that are each broken down into manageable pieces.

---

1. Events are activities that occur that force control flow from one activity to another.

2. Swim lanes are compartments used to separate activities by their object or domain.

3. Forks are used to initiate parallel processing, and joins are used for multiple processes to catch up with others to resume single-processing.

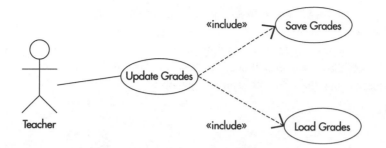

Note that this one use case scenario actually utilizes three use cases. You have not only the Update Grades use case, but also the Save Grades and Load Grades use cases that are included in this functionality. At this time, you should note that these two additional use cases are separated for a reason. If you recall from Module 2, both the Load and Save use cases were reusable functionality being utilized now (or in the future) by other use cases within the use case diagram.

Modeling Primary Paths

When you begin creating an activity diagram for a use case, you want to start with the obvious path through the workflow. From there, you can always expand.

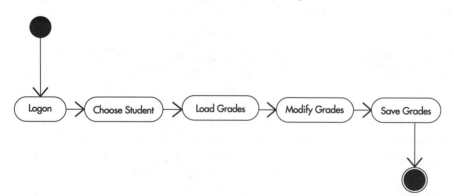

The most obvious path should be the one that takes you from the start to the finish of the workflow with no errors and minimal decision making (this is the easiest path to accomplish the use case). In our situation, the easiest way for a teacher to update grades is to log on, choose a student, load their grades, modify them, and save them.

Modeling Alternative Paths

Now that you have your baseline down, it's time to find your alternative workflow situations. If you take a look at your activity diagram from the previous step, you might begin to envision where the path can lead in other directions that are not modeled yet, perhaps to handle errors, or to perform other activities.

We are now going to add error handling to our activity diagram in the form of a single activity, Display Error, which will occur for just about any error that could occur. This is a critical error, causing the flow of operations to stop.

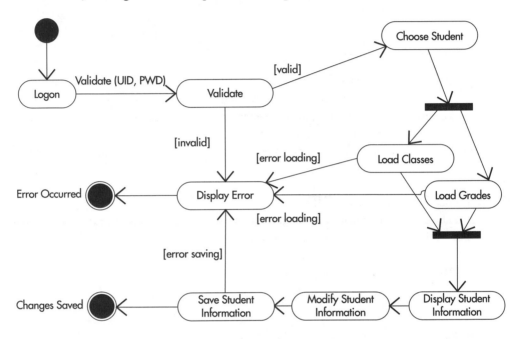

In addition to our error handler, we added some parallel processing to better explain to the reader what we were loading. In this case, we are loading both classes and grades for a student and we would like this to happen at the same time. Because we can't display the user information until we have it, and both pieces of information are being retrieved in their own process, we add a join to wait for the two processes created by the previous fork to catch up to each other.

Adding Swim Lanes

As I said before, I believe that swim lanes are extremely beneficial in reading any activity diagram, and this one is no exception. In this step of our activity diagram modeling, we divided the activities into two swim lanes (see Figure 4-1). The first is the Teacher and the second is the Website. The Teacher is an actor in our use case, but the Website is a generalization of the components that will be providing the backend functionality. Remember that we are in the analysis phase and thus we don't have to model everything with a very low-level design approach. Using these abstract objects will actually give others outside of the development field the opportunity to be able to read and understand your diagrams as well.

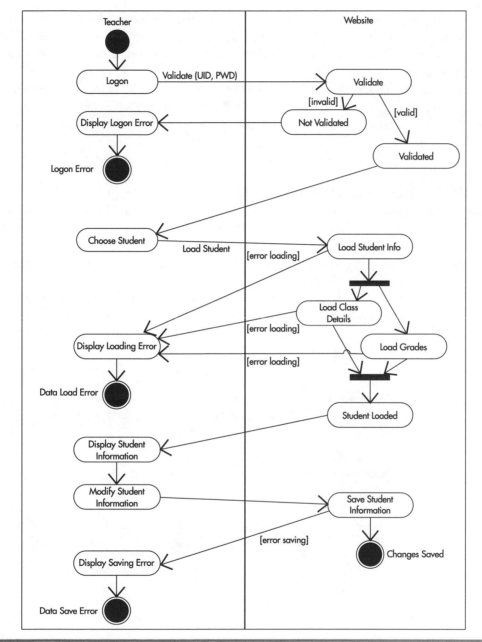

Figure 4-1 Modifying student information with swim lanes

Once again, we have taken this opportunity to iteratively add more detail to our activity diagram. In this case, we have added states to indicate what milestone we are at. After validating the teacher, we set the state to Validated or Not Validated. After loading the student information, we set the state to Student Loaded.

And, finally, we have decided that each error message would be its own activity in our diagram, and thus gave a Logon Error, Data Load Error, and Data Save Error. We could have just as easily created only one activity and let all the error transitions flow to that, but we decided against it.

Refining High-Level Activities

The final step in modeling activity diagrams emphasizes the point of iterative modeling. In this step, you go back to the diagram and make it more detailed. In most cases, you would go back to your diagrams and pick the most complicated activities, whether it be one or all of them. With these complex activities, you would spend time modeling each as their own activity diagram, complete with start and finish states.

In the case of our grading system activity diagram, we realize that the activity, Load Student Info, is vague and really has a lot of functionality behind it.

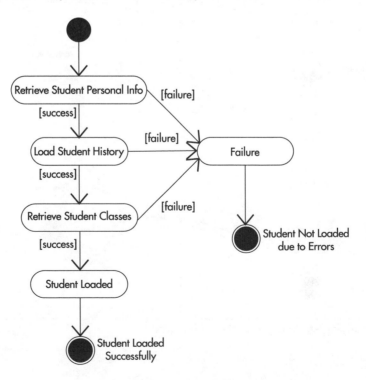

In this case, we model three detailed activities for this single activity. When the Load Student Info activity is initiated from the main activity diagram, we can jump to the preceding smaller diagram to determine that the control flow will move from Retrieve Student Personal Info to Load Student History to Retrieve Student Classes before the Student Loaded state is set and the control flow exits the diagram. Assuming that there were no errors during the processing of these three activities, control flow would continue from the Load Student Info activity onward toward the fork in the main activity diagram so that the student's detailed information could be loaded.

If, however, there was an error within the Load Student Info activity diagram, the state of the activity would be set to Failure and control would pass not to the fork in the main activity diagram, but instead to the Display Loading Error activity, followed by a termination of control flow.

Project 4-2 Model an Activity Diagram

```
Project4-2_Step2.gif
Project4-2_Step3.gif
Project4-2_Step4.gif
```

In this project, you will work from the following use case (taken from the solution to Project 2-2) and create an activity diagram for the workflow represented. You will leverage your knowledge of UML notation for activity diagrams, including the use of activities, states, transitions, conditions, swim lanes, forks, and joins. In addition, when you have created your activity diagram, you will pick the Update Inventory activity and model it separately in a more detailed activity diagram.

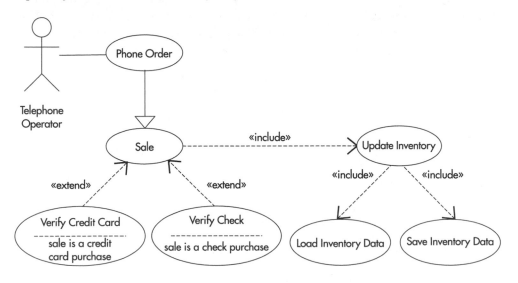

(continued)

Step by Step

1. Step 1 is done, because your use case has already been chosen for you.

2. Model the primary workflow path of the use case.

 NOTE

To assist you in checking your progress on this project, diagrams for selected steps are available online at www.osborne.com. You can easily identify the diagrams available online by referencing the filenames listed with this project's title.

3. Model alternative paths, including error handling, while providing more detail to the original activity diagram.

4. Add swim lanes to your diagram to enhance the readability, and to provide even more detail to the original activity diagram.

5. Provide detail for the Update Inventory activity, which entails quite a bit of processing.

Project Summary

This project really drew upon your abilities to understand, read, and model multiple UML diagram types. You first had to be able to interpret the use case, which became your requirements for your activity diagram. From there, you determined all possible workflows through the use case and modeled them accordingly. If this was completed successfully, you should have concluded with an activity diagram similar to that shown next.

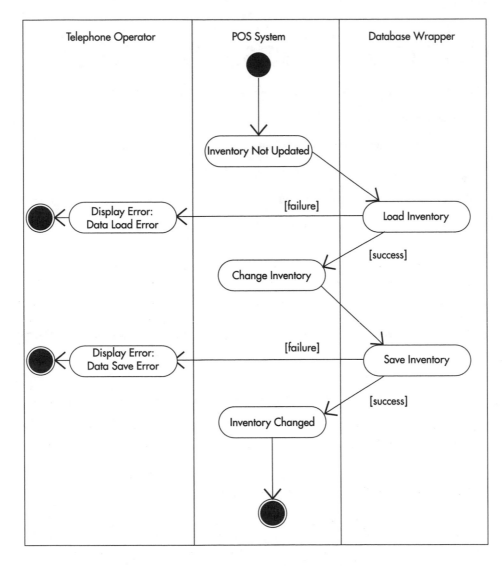

This project also emphasized the requirement of the Unified Process to engage in iterative modeling cycles, as the models were enhanced more and more with each stage until complete.

Module 4 Mastery Check

1. Model an activity diagram for the use case of a driver starting a car.

2. Name some valid states of a file object.

3. What are the notational components of an activity diagram and what are their purposes?

4. What is the difference between guards and triggers?

5. Name the different workflows that might be modeled for the use case of buying a book online.

6. List some activities for the use case to add an e-mail address to a newsgroup list.

7. What is the difference between using conditions and forks?

8. What do swim lanes illustrate to the reader?

9. What are the steps to modeling an activity diagram?

10. What are the advantages of using decision points rather than just guards in an activity model?

Module 5

Modeling Behavior with Sequence Diagrams

At this time, you should have your use cases written and be ready to start modeling your system. To do that, you will first learn about sequence diagrams, which are models that will allow you to show how your actors interact with objects of your system in a series of sequential steps.

CRITICAL SKILL
5.1 # Define Sequence Diagrams

The sequence diagram is one of two types of interaction diagrams. The other is the collaboration diagram, which is covered in Module 7. Sequence diagrams are used to model object interactions arranged in time sequence and to distribute use case behavior to classes. Sequence diagrams are used throughout the software development lifecycle as described in the Unified Process. As you are still in the domain modeling and analysis portion of this book, you will use sequence diagrams that depict the interactions of the actors and objects at a very high level. Later, when you get into the specific design of your system, you will learn some advanced techniques, in Module 9, to really clarify your sequence diagrams.

This module focuses on the basic notational items of the sequence diagram and how you can use it to further develop the analysis provided by the use case and activity diagrams.

CRITICAL SKILL
5.2 # Discover Why We Model Sequence Diagrams

There are a number of specific reasons for modeling sequence diagrams, which, arguably, have the same role as activity diagrams (described in Module 4). One of the reasons, shared by activity diagrams, is to realize a use case. Any one of the use cases that you designed and modeled in Module 2 can be further clarified and realized by a sequence diagram. In fact, sequence diagrams, just like activity diagrams, are used to provide the missing explanation of the generalized function that is specified by a particular use case. For instance, Compile Application was a use case that we modeled in Module 2. This is a very generic description of the functionality. Although necessary in this form to model all the business requirements of a system, and to provide the highest level of understanding of what a system does, it does little to help us move toward the design phase. More analysis has to be done on this use case to provide enough information for design.

A sequence diagram can also be used to illustrate all the paths that a particular use case can ultimately produce, just like an activity diagram. Consider again the Compile Application use case. Sequence diagrams can be modeled to illustrate all possible outcomes of compiling an application. Take a moment to think of all the possible workflows for this use case. Besides the obvious, successfully compiling the application, we can come up with at least the following:

- The project file isn't found

- The source files aren't found

- There are one or more syntax problems in the source files

- There are one or more dependency problems in the source files

- The linker executable can't be found

- The linker fails for some reason

- There is a file input/output error

Each one of these cases can provide for a reason to complete a separate sequence diagram. Now is a good time to reflect on how useful modeling is to the development of software. If you were actually developing a compiler, you would have every last detail specified for you, including each of these error conditions. Without modeling, chances are you will code for each one of these if, and only if, you encounter these problems during development and testing. Chances are even greater that when you develop for these problems, you will not use common reusable source code to handle the error checking, error reporting, and so on.

CRITICAL SKILL
5.3 Identify the Notational Components of Sequence Diagram

A sequence diagram has two major components: active objects and the communications between these active objects. *Active objects* are any objects that play a role in the system, whether that be an object instance or an actor.

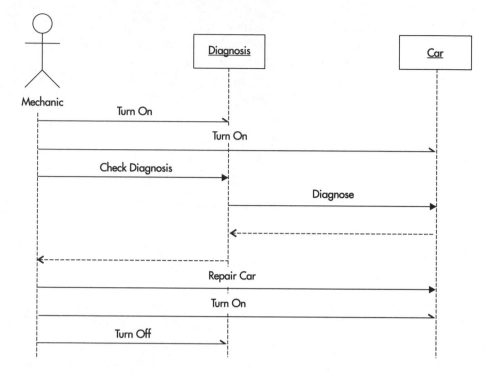

The messages sent between the active objects are the key to sequence diagrams. They illustrate the flow between the objects, how they interact, and what conditions change the flow.

Progress Check

1. What are the two types of interaction diagrams?

2. What are the two components of a sequence diagram?

3. What do sequence diagrams model?

---

1. Sequence and collaboration diagrams
2. Active objects and messages
3. Interaction between different active objects

Active Objects

As just stated, active objects can be actors of a system or any object that is valid within the system. You'll remember from Module 3 that an object is an instance of a class and is drawn with a box surrounding the name. The name is displayed underlined, such as <u>ObjectA</u>. Classes and objects will be covered in more detail in Module 6, but for now, this is sufficient information to begin sequence diagramming.

The notation for objects in the sequence diagram is as follows.

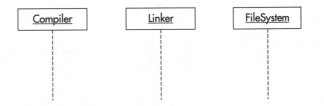

The long dashed line trailing the object is called its *lifeline.* A lifeline will be used to illustrate what is happening to an object in a chronological fashion.

Returning to our Compile Application use case, we would choose a couple of objects that would be interacting with each other and diagram them to begin our sequence diagrams.

As you can see, the objects are drawn from left to right, each with its own lifeline. This type of diagram is notorious for taking up plenty of horizontal space. It is often helpful to model your sequence diagrams in landscape, rather than portrait mode, so that you have more room to work. In fact, if you have legal size paper, you might want to use that.

Messages

Messages are used to illustrate communication between different active objects of a sequence diagram. When an object needs to kick off a process of a different object, or when an object needs to give information to another object, messages are used.

A message is diagramed as an arrow from the calling active object's lifeline to the recipient's lifeline. Above the arrow is the message that is being sent.

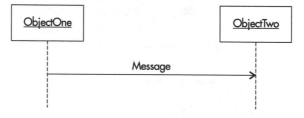

Remember that actors can also be used in sequence diagrams. In fact, illustrating actors as active objects models how actors interact with the system and how the system interacts with the user. Actors can call objects and objects can notify actors.

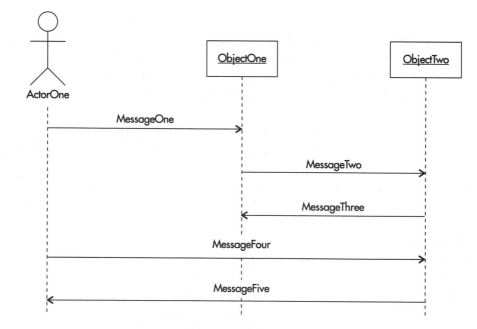

Reading this sequence diagram, we follow the flow of the messages down the timeline, always starting with the topmost message, which starts at ActorOne:

● ActorOne sends MessageOne to ObjectOne

● ObjectOne sends MessageTwo to ObjectTwo

- ObjectTwo sends MessageThree to ObjectOne

- ActorOne sends MessageFour to ObjectTwo

- ObjectTwo sends MessageFive to ActorOne

The last illustration also shows that actors and objects can send messages to any other actor or object in the sequence diagram. They can send messages to actors and objects that are not their immediately adjacent neighbor.

Let's take a look at an example that might make a little more sense. Once again visiting our Compile Application use case, we can create a sequence diagram for the workflow of successfully compiling a project that would fall under the Compile Application use case.

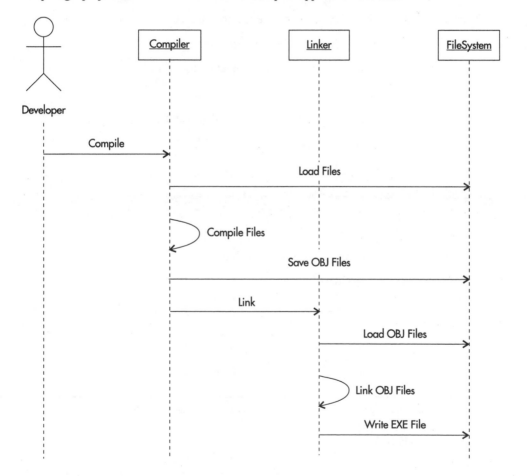

In this sequence diagram, we have four active objects, Developer, Compiler, Linker, and FileSystem. Developer is the actor using the system. The Compiler is the application that the Developer interacts with. The Linker is a separate process that is used to link object files, and the FileSystem is a wrapper around system-level functionality used to perform file input/output routines.

Let's walk through this sequence diagram as we did with the previous one:

- The Developer asks the Compiler to compile

- The Compiler asks the FileSystem to load the files

- The Compiler tells itself to compile

- The Compiler asks the FileSystem to save the object code

- The Compiler asks the Linker to link the object code

- The Linker asks the FileSystem to load the object code

- The Linker tells itself to link

- The Linker asks the FileSystem to save the compiled result

Progress Check

1. What is a lifeline?

2. How do active objects communicate with each other?

3. What are valid active objects?

---

1. A dashed line extending vertically from an active object depicting time over the active object's life
2. With messages
3. Actors and objects (class instances)

CRITICAL SKILL
5.4 Understand How to Use
Messages for Communication

Messages are how active objects communicate with each other in sequence diagrams. There is no other way. You can bet your last dollar that the drafters of UML came up with some neat notation for messaging.

Messages can contain conditions that restrict them from being sent unless met. A condition is shown in brackets directly above the name of the message.

The following example of message conditions shows how a sequence diagram can be modeled to show a login attempt. If the login fails, it is retried once before giving up.

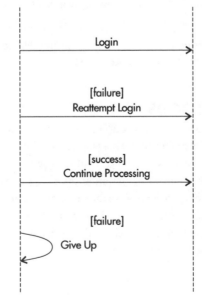

So far in this section, you have seen only one type of message, which is called a flat message. There are four message types in total:

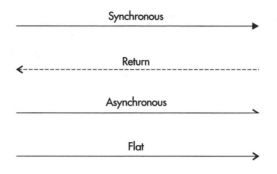

- ● **Synchronous**   Indicates that flow is interrupted until the message has completed, and any messages that were sent from that message are completed as well. Synchronous messages are modeled with a solid arrow and line.

- ● **Return**   Shows that control flow has returned to the calling active object, and that the synchronous message has completed its operation. Return messages are modeled as a dashed line with an open arrow.

- ● **Asynchronous**   Used for messages that are sent, but from which the active object doesn't wait for a response. Asynchronous messages are modeled as a solid line with half an open arrow.

- ● **Flat**   Makes no distinction between synchronous and asynchronous. Flat messages are modeled as a solid line with an open arrow.

Synchronous Messages

Synchronous messages are used for procedural system flow where one piece of functionality is executed before another. The synchronous message is used when it is important that a message is received and completed before execution or control flow continues.

In the following illustration, the Teacher attempts to log in to the Web Interface. The login and subsequent calls are synchronous because they rely on the previous messages. Specifically, the Lookup Student Info message can't execute unless the Login Teacher message was successful. Notice the use of the return messages that show the user when and where the control flow is handed over. The Teacher sends the Login Teacher message to the Web Interface, which in turn sends the Validate User message to the Database Wrapper functionality. Then, control is returned first to the Web Interface, which then returns control to the Teacher with information that would indicate whether or not the login was successful.

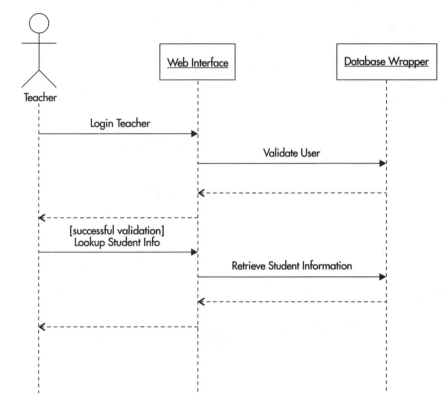

Asynchronous Messages

Asynchronous messages are used when control flow does not need to be interrupted before completing. Some examples of messages that may be considered for asynchronous status are messages that indicate information should be saved (if it is not being read immediately), notification of somebody or something, or even messages that post progress information.

The following example illustrates how asynchronous messages can be used in a log file scenario. This sequence diagram shows the Teacher logging in to the grading system and checking a student's grades. For security reasons, we have a log file that records every move made by a user. There is no reason for the rest of the application and process to wait for the log file to be written to, so these messages are sent asynchronously.

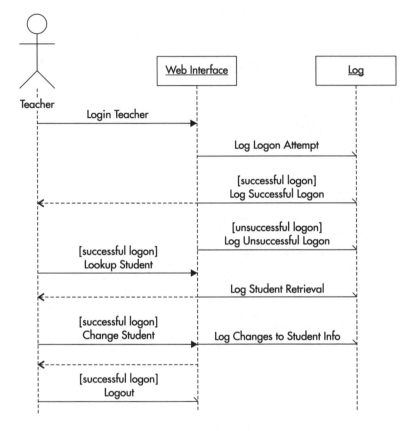

Flat Messages

If every message is synchronous or asynchronous, then why do we have flat messages? Because sometimes we don't care and sometimes we don't know. In high-level analyses, it may not be important to specify whether a message is asynchronous or synchronous. In other cases, as shown in the next example, we may never know.

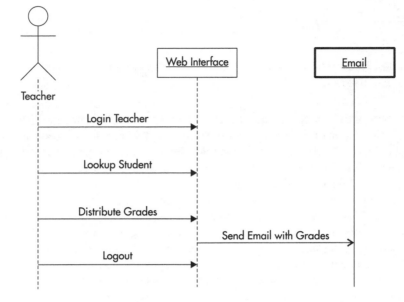

This example shows that the Teacher logs in to the Web Interface to distribute a student's grades electronically, via an e-mail message. Here, the e-mail component is not part of our system; it is an external component that we communicate to with standard interfaces. The standard interfaces, depending upon how they are implemented, may wait for completion before returning to the client or may return focus immediately.

Notice that the Email active object is shown with a heavy border. This indicates that it is a separate process that has its own control flow and does not depend upon the current system's control flow.

Progress Check

1. How is specific information passed from one active object to another?

2. What do synchronous and asynchronous mean?

3. What is the purpose of a message condition?

---

1. With messages.

2. Synchronous means one at a time, while asynchronous means multiple at the same time.

3. A message condition only allows the message to be sent if the condition is True.

Ask the Expert

Q: How do I know when to model an activity diagram and when to model a sequence diagram?

A: While both activity and sequence diagrams appear to give the same information, they express the information completely differently. As you have already seen, a sequence diagram focuses more on the objects and actors involved in a system and how they interact with each other. An activity diagram, on the other hand, focuses on the functionality and the steps from one activity to another.

It could probably be argued that any sequence diagram can be modeled as an activity diagram and vice versa. However, depending upon the model, you may find one diagramming technique more appropriate than another. In some cases, you may use both.

Consider, for instance, a very high-level use case such as Process Exchange for a retail store. You may decide to create a sequence diagram to model the interaction and workflow between the Salesclerk, the Customer, and the system used to process the exchange. Then, once you have this completed, you may decide that within this sequence diagram are fairly complex tasks that need to be modeled on their own. You can then use one or more activity diagrams to break the sequence diagram into more detail.

Whatever you do—you won't be wrong. Pick the diagram that best communicates the intent of the system.

CRITICAL SKILL
5.5 Learn Other Techniques
Used in Sequence Diagrams

Now that you understand the basic notation of a sequence diagram, we can add more functionality to your bag of tricks. Until now, your sequence diagrams all have had objects that were already created when the sequence diagram took life. In this section, you will learn how you can create objects on-the-fly within your diagrams. Just as with activity diagrams, you can set the state of the object that has control within sequence diagrams. Also, just as with activity diagrams, there are ways to change the control flow of sequence diagrams by branching and using alternative flows.

Creating Objects

The notation for creating an object on-the-fly is shown in the following example. There is one mandatory step and that is to send the «create» message to the body of the object instance. Once the object is created, it is given a lifeline, just like any other object in the sequence diagram. You can now send and receive messages with this object as you can with any other object in the sequence diagram. When you are done with the newly created object, or any other object in the sequence diagram for that matter, you can send the «destroys» message to remove it. To indicate that an object has been destroyed, you want to place an X on the lifeline where it is destroyed. At that point, there is no reason to continue extending the lifeline downward.

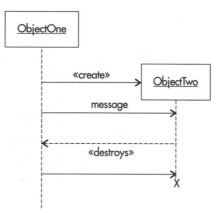

An object can be created during the flow of a sequence diagram for many reasons. The one that I use a lot is to create notifications to the user. In this case, we use an object, such as a message box, to display an error to the user, and then we destroy it when we are done with it.

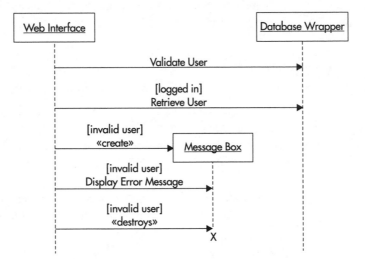

In reality, you can use this functionality for anything that you do. You can open database connections, create instances of data classes, or even create files.

Using States

States belong to objects and exist directly on the lifeline of their objects. States can be set and exist prior to any messages in a sequence diagram, or they can be set by other objects within the diagram, as shown in the following notational explanation.

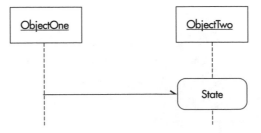

In the next example, we combine the creation of objects on-the-fly and the use of states to show how a Web Interface and Database Wrapper can create a User Information object and populate it. The states within the User Information object indicate whether or not the data that belongs to it has been saved since it was modified.

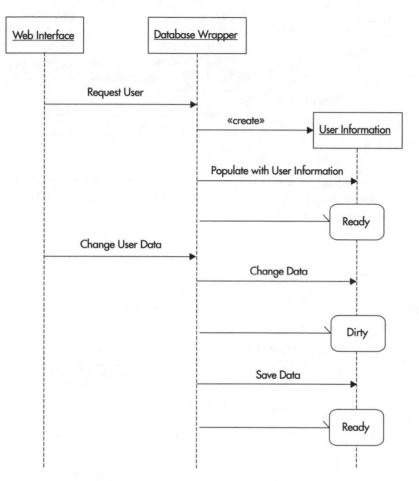

Branching and Alternative Flows

There are two ways for sequence diagrams to change their control flow: with branching and with alternative flows. Both are very similar, but each has a slightly different notation. Changes in the control flow occur when different conditions cause the flow to go separate ways.

Branching allows for the flow to go to different objects.

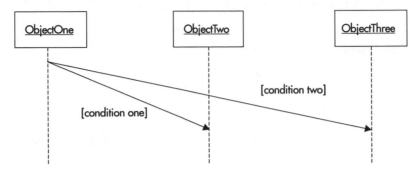

Notice that the starting location for the messages is the same and the ending "height" for the branched messages is equivalent. This indicates that in the next step, one of these will be executed, as in the following example:

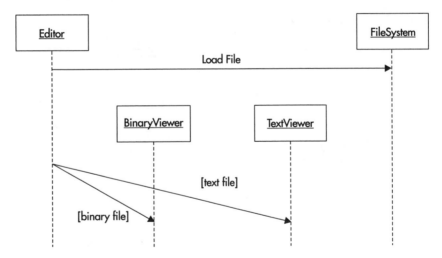

The Editor application attempts to open a file using the object that best fits the file type. If the file is binary, a binary viewer object is used; otherwise, if it is a text file, the text viewer object is used.

Alternative flow also allows the control flow to change based upon conditions, but it allows the flow to change to an alternative lifeline branch of the same object.

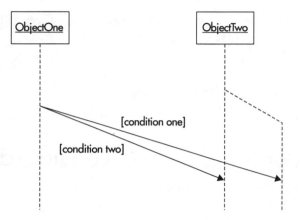

In the next example, the Editor sends a message to the FileSystem if the user deletes a file or saves a file. Obviously, the FileSystem is going to perform two very different activities and will require separate lifelines for each flow.

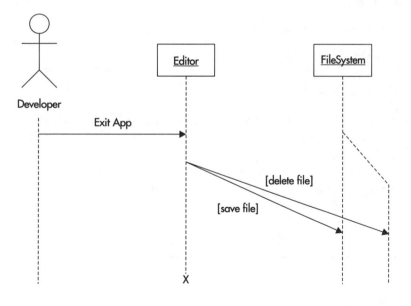

Progress Check

1. What is the name of the message to create an object within a sequence diagram? What about the message to remove it?

2. To what do states belong?

3. What are the two types of control flow changes?

Project 5-1 Reading a Sequence Diagram

In this project, you will read the sequence diagram shown in Figure 5-1 that explains the steps for a developer to compile an application. While reading the diagram, identify the notational components that you have learned so far.

Step by Step

1. Identify the actors and the objects of the diagram.

2. Identify where the error handling occurs.

3. Identify the messages in the order of control flow.

Project Summary

This project proved that you could read a sequence diagram from the first message to the last. You should have been able to identify messages, such as the Linker tells itself to Link, and the Editor tells the Message Box to display Compiler Complete. You should have been able to identify the control flow changes for error conditions and you should have identified that the actors and objects included Developer, Editor, and Linker.

---

1. «create», «destroys»
2. Objects
3. Branching and alternative flows

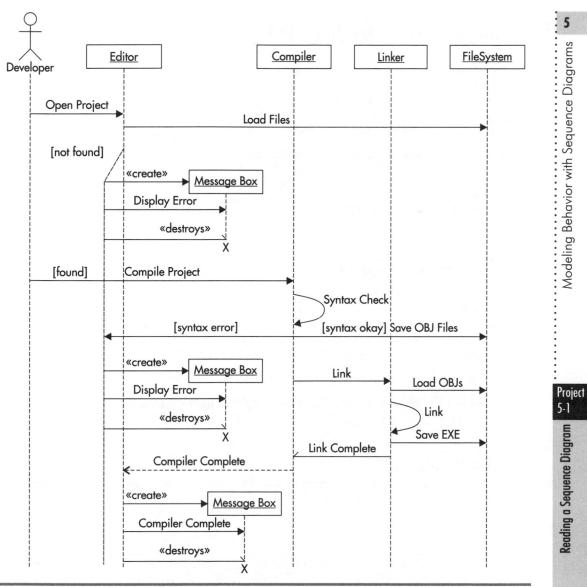

Figure 5-1 Compiling an application

CRITICAL SKILL
5.6
Learn How to Model Sequence Diagrams

There are four tasks for creating sequence diagrams:

1. Decide on the workflows that you will model.

2. Lay out your objects from left to right.

3. Include messages and conditions to build each workflow.

4. Draw a generic diagram to combine the separate diagrams.

As we go through each step, we will draw from your knowledge of the sequence diagram notation and the Unified Process as an iterative process.

Decide on Workflows

The first step in modeling your sequence diagram is to decide on the workflows you are going to model. For the purpose of this exercise, we are going to model the View Grades use case of a the Grading System. In doing this, we identify at least three workflows that we should model:

● The teacher views the grades for a student successfully.

● The teacher attempts to view the grades for a student, but the student doesn't exist in the system.

● The teacher attempts to view the grades for a student, but the student does not have any grades in the system.

Lay Out Objects

The next step in modeling your sequence diagram is to lay out all of your actors and objects from left to right, and include their lifelines for you to begin adding messages to.

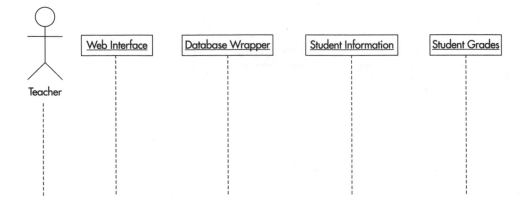

This illustration only shows one set of actors and objects, but you will want to do this three times, one for each workflow that you are going to model.

Include Messages and Conditions

Next, you begin modeling each workflow as a separate sequence diagram. Start with the basic workflow, which is the one without any error conditions and the least amount of decisions. In this case, the basic workflow is the teacher viewing the grades for a student successfully.

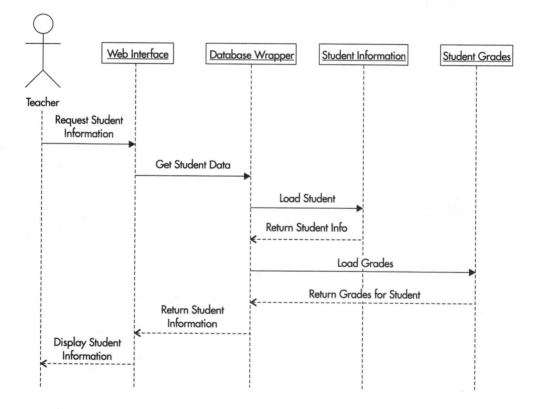

Remember to choose your message types wisely (asynchronous, synchronous, flat, and return). Continue by modeling the alternative workflows as stand-alone diagrams. Only model the negative conditions.

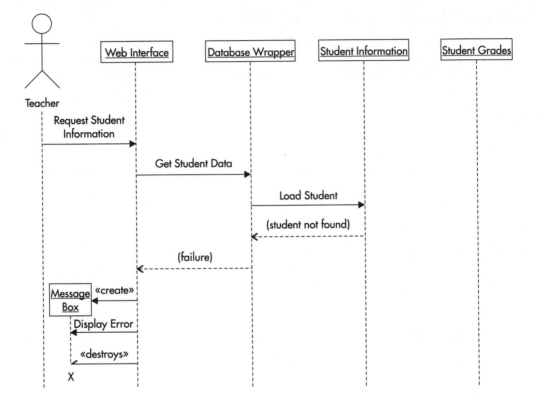

Remember to use conditions to indicate which messages are to be sent at which time.

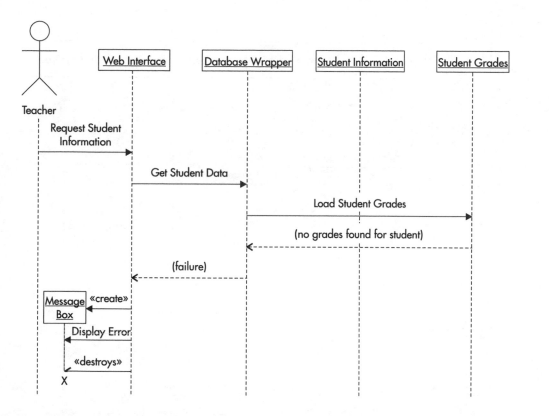

Now you should have completed sequence diagrams for each of your workflows.

Draw a Generic Diagram

The final step in modeling a sequence diagram is to combine each individual workflow into a single, generic workflow, as shown in Figure 5-2.

At this stage, you can generalize some early messages and interaction if you feel it is too detailed for the current diagram, but if you do, you may want to keep the original individual diagrams to enhance clarification for the next stage of software modeling.

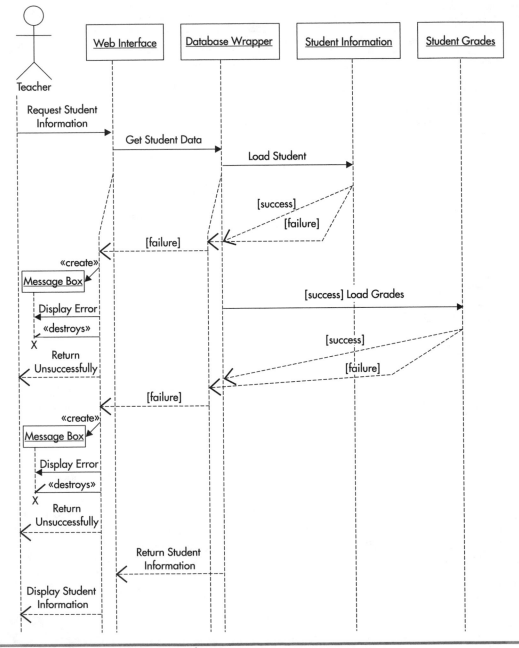

Figure 5-2 The generic sequence diagram

Project 5-2 Modeling a Sequence Diagram

Project5-2_Step2.gif
Project5-2_Step3a.gif
Project5-2_Step3b.gif

In this project, you will create a sequence diagram for the use case of removing an item from inventory after a sale. You will leverage your knowledge of the UML notation for sequence diagrams, including messaging and message types, conditions, states, branching, and alternative flows.

Step by Step

1. Identify the workflows that you will model as separate sequence diagrams.

2. Lay out your objects for the individual sequence diagrams.

NOTE

To assist you in checking your progress on this project, diagrams for selected steps are available online at www.osborne.com. You can easily identify the diagrams available online by referencing the filenames listed with this project's title.

3. Include messages and conditions for your individual sequence diagrams.

4. Model a common, generic sequence diagram from the individual diagrams.

Project Summary

In this project, you proved your knowledge of the UML notation for sequence diagrams and your understanding of the Unified Process as you applied iterative diagramming to your model. You should have successfully diagrammed multiple workflows, both basic (successful) and alternative (error condition) within a single generic sequence diagram. If completed successfully, you should have ended up with a diagram that looks similar to what's shown in Figure 5-3.

(continued)

Project
5-2

Modeling a Sequence Diagram

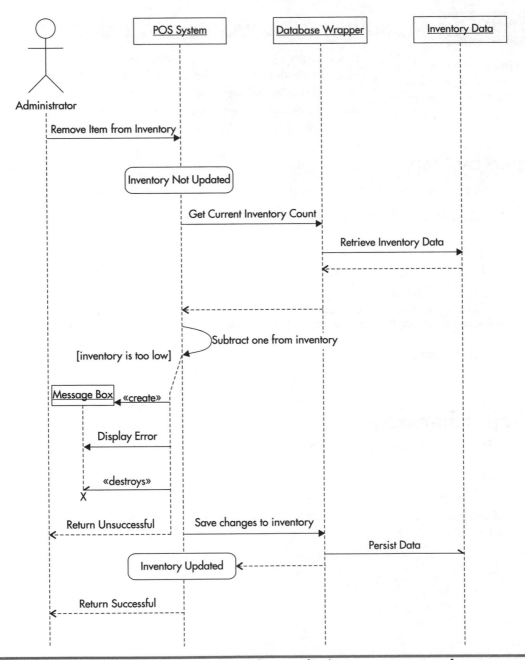

Figure 5-3 The completed generic sequence diagram for the Removing an Item from Inventory After a Sale use case

Module 5 Mastery Check

1. Why are sequence diagrams modeled?

2. What are the four types of messages and what are the differences between each of them?

3. Model the creation of a database object, the connection of that object to a data source, and the query of the object for a resultset.

4. To what do states belong?

5. What are the four steps to modeling a sequence diagram?

6. What are some differences between use case diagrams and sequence diagrams?

7. What is the difference between synchronous and asynchronous messages?

8. Identify some alternative workflows for taking money out of an ATM machine.

9. What are the types of active objects that can be used in a sequence diagram?

10. What are the two keywords used when instantiating an object within a sequence diagram?

Module 6

Defining Domain Models Using Class Diagrams

The basis to object-oriented design is the use of classes. Classes are building blocks that are used to represent real-world items or functionality. In this module, you will learn how to model classes and their relationships to each other, to begin forming the overall picture of your system before you touch a line of code.

Define Class Diagrams

Class diagrams are static diagrams consisting of pieces that make up our system or subsystem. Class diagrams are modeled throughout the analysis and the design stages of a project, starting with classes that business folk may understand, but most certainly ending up with classes that are only comprehensible to the development team. Class diagrams are essential to any project that is object-oriented, as we discussed in Module 3. As you will recall, classes contain attributes and operations that allow them to obtain state and to provide functionality. Later in this module, we will be illustrating how to model attributes and operations for classes.

Classes have relationships with other classes, which, when combined, form the paths described in the activity and sequence diagrams that you have modeled in the previous two modules. In this module, we will focus on how class diagrams are created from use case diagrams to supplement and fulfill the activity and sequence diagrams that describe paths, by providing a means to achieve these paths.

Discover Why We Model Class Diagrams

We model class diagrams to show more detail about our product. Modeling class diagrams is an iterative process just like modeling any other diagram of the UML according to the Unified Process. Usually, class diagrams begin with a high-level overview of the functionality that the final application will provide, but the classes that belong to these early models are very rarely the classes that are used in the final product to provide low-level functionality such as data access and communication. As the system's class diagrams mature, growing in number and size, they become more detailed, showing every path that a stream of execution in a product can take—giving the product a good map of where to go to find the functionality that it requires. We model class diagrams to give us the information we need to put together this map. This map is formed by individual classes and their relationships to each other.

We also diagram class diagrams to indicate where data resides and where functionality is available through the use of class attributes and operations. The attributes and operations that are exposed to other classes make up the public class interface. This is the data and functionality that is available to outside classes. In a similar matter, we can use class diagrams to indicate which paths are available to existing class packages such as third-party tools, or an existing system.

CRITICAL SKILL
6.3 Identify the Notational Components of Class Diagrams

A class diagram consists of classes and their relationships to each other. Classes can contain attributes and operations. They can have relationships with other classes and can include something called multiplicity, which you will learn about shortly.

Chances are that you can read the following illustration of a class diagram with little confusion. We are going to make sure that you have no confusion at all when it comes to this diagram, and diagrams like it, by explaining the basic notation for class diagramming.

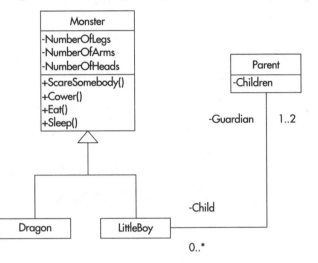

Classes

Classes are the meat of class diagrams, as you probably already figured out. Remember that in Module 3, we said that a class is a representation of a generalized thing, such as an animal, a person, a car, a ticket, or a system. A class can have state (recorded through the use of its own data—called attributes) and provide functionality (through the use of its operations or methods). In the previous illustration, the classes that were included were the Monster, Dragon, LittleBoy, and Parent classes.

In Module 3, we said that classes are designed to be self-contained through the use of encapsulation. This is true for the most part. Classes should be self-contained in the following respects:

● *They should encapsulate only the information and functionality that is important to them.* In the previous illustration, the Monster class includes attributes that contain values for how many arms, legs, and heads monsters have, but it doesn't contain values for the bus schedule, or the price of a hamburger—these are clearly pieces of information that do not pertain to the Monster class. Similarly, the Monster class does not have operations that provide functionality to behave or clean their room—because clearly monsters do not do that.

● *They should encapsulate all the information and functionality that is important to them in the context of the system.* This means that if our system was a scaring system, and a monster scares, the Monster class should have functionality to scare. If the system has nothing to do with scaring, but instead has to do with playing, then scaring would have no place in the Monster class. This would be considered overkill in this system…and the last thing you need a monster to do is overkill.

Progress Check

1. Why do we model class diagrams?

2. What are the two main components of classes?

3. What other UML diagrams do we use to model class diagrams from?

Now that you understand what classes contain, let's take a look at the formal notation of a class.

ClassName
-attribute1 -attribute2 -attribute3
+operation1() +operation2() +operation3()

As you can see, the class notation consists of a box divided into three compartments. The first compartment always contains the name of the class. The second compartment lists the attributes (data), and the third compartment lists the operations (functionality).

---

1. To show more detail about our product and to show the information needed to put together a map indicating the paths through the available functionality

2. Attributes and operations

3. Activity and sequence diagrams

The following illustration shows three examples of classes that are totally independent of one another.

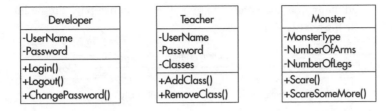

The Teacher class has the functionality to add and remove classes through the operations listed in the third compartment of the class notation. It also provides the attributes, or data, to hold a username, password, and the classes for that teacher. These are all listed in the second compartment of the class notation.

Relationships

Two classes can relate to each other with a line and an association name.

A pointer that shows the direction of the association follows the association name. If the association name was replaced with the text "owns >" in the preceding notation, it would be read as "ClassOne owns ClassTwo." If the association name were replaced with "< owns," then, according to the notation, it would read as "ClassTwo owns ClassOne" or "ClassOne is owned by ClassTwo."

In the following illustration, you can see that the Teacher *teaches* a Class or, equivalently, a Class is *taught by* a Teacher. It also shows that a Student *takes* a Class, or a Class is *taken by* a Student.

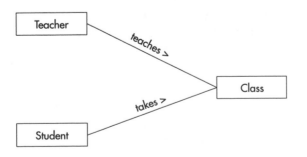

Multiplicity

Multiplicity allows us to indicate how many objects of one class relate to one object of another class. We can add multiplicity on either end of a class relationship by simply indicating it next to the class where the relationship enters.

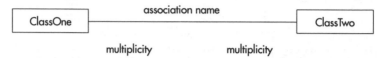

Multiplicity is a single number or a range of numbers, indicating how many objects of that class relate to one object of another class. The use of a single number means that there is always exactly that number of objects of that class, such as 1, 2, or 3.

A range of numbers can be shown by indicating a minimum number, two periods (..), and then a maximum number. For instance, 1..3 means one to three objects relate to one object of the other class. The notation 0..5 means anywhere from zero to five objects of one class are related to the object of the other class. The maximum number can be replaced by an asterisk, which represents an unlimited number of objects, usually read as "many." One to many objects is represented as 1..*, and 0..* reads zero to many (or any number of).

In the following illustration, we see that a Teacher teaches one to many classes. A Teacher has to have at least one class, but the Teacher can have up to an unlimited number of classes (which of course is not really fair). Reading the class diagram the other way, we see that a Class has one and only one Teacher.

Taking the previous example to the next step, we can add multiplicity to the Student/Class relationship. Here we see that a Student takes 4 to 6 classes, and a Class has 10 to 30 students.

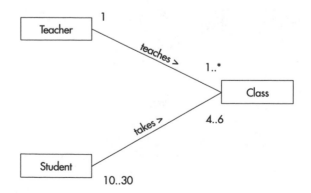

TIP

Multiplicity can also be used to show multiple groups of ranges and numbers, such as 1, 3..*, meaning 1 or 3 to many, which in turn ultimately means any number but 2. Another example would be 2, 4, 8, 10, which would mean any even number up to ten.

Roles

Our class relationships can be further beefed up by adding roles. The use of a role in a class diagram helps the reader to understand what the first class does for the second. A role is shown in the same place as the multiplicity, either above or below the line indicating the relationship where it enters the class.

```
                        association name

          rolename1              rolename2
ClassOne ───────────────────────────────── ClassTwo

          multiplicity            multiplicity
```

In this notation, a role name can be incorporated into the reading of a relationship to indicate "ClassOne plays the role of *rolename1* for ClassTwo" and "ClassTwo plays the role of *rolename2* for ClassOne."

The next illustration shows an example of how a single class, Teacher, can play two roles in separate relationships with a single Class.

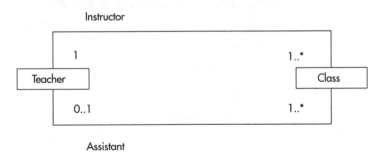

From this class diagram, we can deduct that "A Class has one Teacher who plays the role of the Instructor" and "A Class has zero or one Teacher who plays the role of the Assistant."

Progress Check

1. Which compartment are class operations listed in?

2. What does the multiplicity of 1..5, 7, 9..* indicate?

3. Identify the classes, roles, and multiplicity in the relationship "A developer has one or more computers that play the role of their build machine."

CRITICAL SKILL

6.4 Learn What Makes a Class

When modeling a class in UML, you have a lot of flexibility. The same class can be modeled in four different ways:

● With no attributes or operations shown

● With only the attributes shown

● With only the operations shown

● With both the attributes and operations shown

The name of the class is always in the first compartment of the class box; in fact, it is the only required component, as we have seen in the many previous examples.

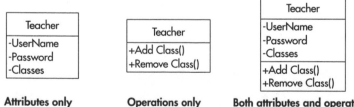

Attributes only   **Operations only**   **Both attributes and operations**

(We've seen already how a class is modeled with only the class name—just a rectangle with the name of the class.)

UML gives us plenty of flexibility when modeling classes for a very good reason. As you will see as you continue to model your classes, the list of attributes and operations that a class can and

---

1. The third compartment

2. 1 to 5, 7, or 9 to many—or any number greater than zero and not 6 or 8

3. Classes: Developer and Computer; Roles: A computer plays the role of a Build Machine; Multiplicity: There are 1..* computers.

will have can be tremendous. A class can model not only its public attributes and operations, but also its private attributes and operations. Private members like these are used only by the class that they belong to. They usually are included in order to provide functionality and data that will ultimately be exposed by a public member of the class interface.

When the list of operations and attributes grows large, a single class can be overwhelming to a model, especially when that class is not the main focus of the model. Remember, you can model as many class diagrams as you wish in order to express the design of your system. Choose wisely when to display the members that are important to the diagram that you are modeling.

There is one very important thing to keep in mind when hiding member attributes and operations—when you hide the compartment, the reader of the diagram does not know if operations and attributes exist. Hiding, or suppressing, a compartment means you don't display the box that they are listed in at all. This is very different from leaving the compartments empty.

In the following illustration, the first class does not display compartments for the attributes or the operations, which does not tell the user whether or not they exist. The second class does something completely different—it tells the user that there are no operations and no attributes. Be careful how you draw your classes.

ClassName

Attributes and operations
are hidden

ClassName

No attributes or operations
in the class

Attributes and Operations

As you have learned, attributes are used to represent pieces of data that are specific to a class and ultimately give it state. When modeling attributes in a class, they are located in the second compartment of the class box if you decide to show the reader that there are attributes associated with a class. If you do not have any attributes belonging to a class, and you want the reader to know this, you should show the second compartment of the class box as empty.

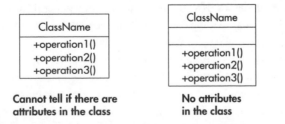

ClassName
+operation1()
+operation2()
+operation3()

Cannot tell if there are
attributes in the class

ClassName
+operation1() +operation2() +operation3()

No attributes
in the class

The preceding illustration shows that there is a difference between not showing the compartment (which does not tell the reader if attributes are available in this class) and showing an empty compartment (which tells the reader that no attributes are available in this class).

6

Defining Domain Models Using Class Diagrams

Operations are used to provide functionality for other classes that relate with the modeled class. Just as with attributes, the operations compartment of the class box can be omitted to suppress the list or can be left empty to indicate that operations do not exist at all in the class.

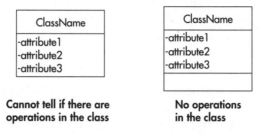

By now, you may be wondering what the plus (+) and minus (-) signs mean in all the class diagrams in this module. So far, all the attributes have been shown with a preceding minus sign, and all the operations have been shown with a preceding plus sign. These two signs indicate the visibility of member attributes and operations. By being visible, a member attribute or operation is available to related classes to access.

The plus sign is used to indicate that a member is visible and can be accessed by an outside, relating class. The minus sign is the opposite, indicating that the member is private to the class and cannot be accessed by outside classes at all. Private attributes and operations are modeled to ensure that business rules are carried out properly and to offer public member operations and attributes assistance in their functionality.

A third sign, the number sign (#), is used to illustrate that the attribute or operation is protected, which means that it is visible to classes of the same system and that classes outside of the current system cannot access it.

There is no difference between attributes and operations when it comes to being visible or not. However, attributes typically are not visible by default, and operations usually are defaulted to visible. Ultimately, when you get further into the design of your class models, you will have both public and private attributes and operations.

Objects: Instances of Classes

Objects are instances of classes. If you think of a class in a general form, such as a Car, an object would be your car or my car. All the cars you would see on the street would be instances, while the mold that was used to make them would be the class.

If you use the classes that we've been working with so far in this model—Developer, Teacher, and Monster—we can think of instances of these classes. For example, the current developer of the system would be an instance of the Developer class, a social studies teacher would be an instance of the Teacher class, and a big monster would be an instance of the Monster class (as compared to a small monster).

The notation for an object is very similar to its class counterpart. It is a box, with the text <u>Object Name : Class Name</u>. A colon separates the object name from the class name, and the entire description is underlined. In the following diagram, the CurrentDeveloper is the name of the instance of the Developer class. Similarly, the SocialStudiesTeacher is an instance of the Teacher class, and the BigMonster is an instance of the Monster class.

```
| CurrentDeveloper : Developer |
```

```
| SocialStudiesTeacher : Teacher |
```

```
| BigMonster : Monster |
```

So what does it mean to be an instance of a class? Simple—an instance of a class has state. It has values for its attributes, making it "unique" in some sense. For instance, one teacher object may have a value of Social Studies for its Subject attribute while another would have Math. Although the object's class, Teacher, has the same attribute, the value of this attribute for each instance gives them state.

Although many objects can have the same attribute values, they can also have very different values. A class has functionality, but it does not have attributes that make it an instance.

When an object has its attribute value modeled, the value is shown after the attribute name with an equal sign (=) between them.

```
| CurrentDeveloper : Developer |
|------------------------------|
| UserName = jroff             |
| Password = jasonrocks        |
```

```
| BigMonster : Monster   |
|------------------------|
| MonsterType = Green    |
| NumberOfArms = 12701   |
| NumberOfLegs = 2       |
```

Attribute values are specified

```
| SocialStudiesTeacher : Teacher |
|--------------------------------|
| UserName                       |
| Password                       |
| Classes                        |
```

Attribute values are not specified

The CurrentDeveloper object is an instance of the Developer class, which has a UserName of jroff and a Password of jasonrocks. The BigMonster object is an instance of the Monster class. It has a MonsterType value of Green, a NumberOfArms value of 12,701, and a NumberOfLegs value of 2. The SocialStudiesTeacher object is an instance of the Teacher class, but none of its attributes are specified in the model. This does not mean that they do not exist or they are not set, it simply means they are not specified. They are not conveyed in this particular model.

Packages

Packages are a way of grouping classes into common categories. Now I'd like to show you how both classes and objects are modeled when specifying the package they belong to. Classes and objects will interact with other classes and objects from different packages—this is how packages are tied together to create a system.

A package is expressed by appending the name of the package and a double colon (::) before the class name in either an object or a class. In the following illustration, the Developer class belongs to the Development package, the Teacher class belongs to the Grading package, and the Monster class belongs to the Scaring package.

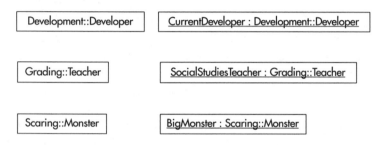

You should always indicate the package of a class when it belongs to a package outside of the package that is being modeled.

Progress Check

1. What is the difference between attributes and operations?

2. What do the attribute and operation predecessors +, -, and # represent?

3. What is a package?

4. Identify the package, object, and class in JasonTRoff : Wackos :: RockStar.

---

1. An attribute is used to represent state information, while an operation is used to perform functionality relating specifically to the class.
2. Public, private, and protected, respectively
3. A way of grouping classes into common categories
4. Wackos is the package, JasonTRoff is the object, and RockStar is the class

CRITICAL SKILL
6.5 Learn How to Give Attributes Detail

Attributes can be so much more than simply a name. You can also specify their data type, give them an initial or default value, give them multiplicity, and even indicate that they are derived from a business rule.

Data Types

The first thing you will want to do when you are detailing your attribute is to indicate what the attribute's data type is. The data type is added after the attribute name, separated by a colon. In the following example, Name is a public attribute that contains a String value, Password is a private attribute that contains a String value, and GradeLevel is a public attribute that contains an Integer value.

Student
+Name : String -Password : String +GradeLevel : Integer

A data type can be anything that you desire, including the following:

- Any standard data type from programming languages such as Visual Basic, C++, C#, and Java
- A class that you have already defined
- A data type from the list of data types within the Interface Definition Language (IDL)
- Something that the reader can comprehend in the scope of the system that you are modeling

Ask the Expert

Q: What are the standard data types?

A: The most common data types usually come from Visual Basic, C++, C#, Java, and IDL. The following tables list the common data types of each. In many cases, the same data type will appear in multiple lists.

Visual Basic Data Types

Boolean	Double	Single
Byte	Integer	String
Currency	Long	Variant
Date	Object	

(continued)

C++ Data Types

bool	long double	unsigned char
char	short	unsigned int
double	signed char	unsigned long
float	signed int	unsigned short
int	signed long	void
long	signed short	wchar_t

C# Data Types

bool	float	short
byte	int	string
char	long	uint
decimal	object	ulong
double	sbyte	ushort

Java Data Types

Boolean	double	long
byte	float	short
char	int	

IDL Data Types

any	long	unsigned long
Boolean	long long	unsigned long long
char	object	unsigned short
double	octet	wchar
fixed	sequence	wstring
float	short	
long double	string	

6

Defining Domain Models Using Class Diagrams

Initial Values

You can specify a default value for an attribute by appending an equal sign (=) and the value after the attribute name and data type.

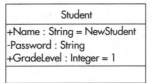

```
          Student
+Name : String = NewStudent
-Password : String
+GradeLevel : Integer = 1
```

Notice that both the Name and GradeLevel attributes have been assigned default values, but the Password attribute was not given one. Setting default values is completely dependent upon the needs of your system—you do not need to do it.

Multiplicity

Multiplicity can also be applied to attributes as it is applied to relationships between classes. Take, for instance, a Student class that has the attribute Grades. You wouldn't want this attribute to contain a single value, but instead you would want it to contain all the grades for that student, which can be any number.

In the following class diagram, we set multiplicity for each attribute even if it is single or one. Notice that Grades has a multiplicity of 0..*, which means any number of grades can be contained within this attribute (zero to many).

```
          Student
+Name[1] : String = NewStudent
-Password[1] : String
+GradeLevel[1] : Integer = 1
+Grades[0..*] : Integer
```

Within an instance of a class, you can specify a value for an attribute that has multiplicity by putting the separate values within curly braces ({ and }) to form a set.

```
          Student
+Name[1] : String = NewStudent
-Password[1] : String
+GradeLevel[1] : Integer = 1
+Grades[0..*] : Integer
```

```
      CurrentStudent : Student
Name : String = Zachary
Password : String = zachrocks
GradeLevel : Integer = 1
Grades : Integer = {90, 95, 87, 45, 100, 99}
```

You can also use the set notation to give an attribute a set of default values within the class itself, although giving students default grades isn't such a good idea.

Derived Attributes

Another interesting thing you can do with attributes is give them a derived value—one that can be derived using math, string functions, or some other business logic that you can later implement in your application.

TIP

We use the term "derive" rather than "calculate" because attributes that are non-numeric can also contain logic for their value. For instance, an attribute called Initials may derive its value from the FirstName, MiddleName, and LastName attributes, all of which will certainly not be numeric.

To indicate that an attribute is derived, you precede its name with a forward slash (/) and attach a note to the attribute with instructions for deriving the attribute value.

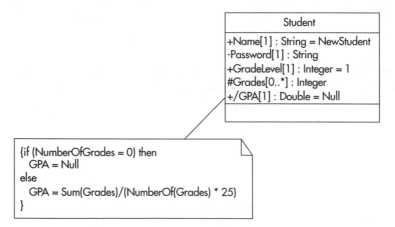

The business logic that is included in a note attached to the derived attribute can contain pseudocode (shown in this example), actual code, a text note, or Object Constraint Language (OCL), which is discussed in Module 12.

Student
+Name[1] : String = NewStudent -Password[1] : String +GradeLevel[1] : Integer = 1 #Grades[0..*] : Integer +/GPA[1] : Double = Null
+AddGrade(in Grade : Integer = 100) +ClearGrades() +ChangePassword(in OldPassword : String, in NewPassword : String) : Boolean

{If (OldPassword = Password Attrbiute) Then
   Password Attribute = NewPassword
   Return Value = True
Else
   Return Value = False}

You can indicate the derived value of an attribute in a class. You can also indicate the current value for an instance of the class, by including it in the object.

In the following example, for our Student class, we have a default value of Null for the derived GPA attribute because we do not have any default values for the Grades attribute. In our class instance for CurrentStudent, the grades of 90, 95, 87, 45, 100, and 99 give the derived GPA attribute a value of 3.44 according to the derived notation's business logic.

Student
+Name[1] : String = NewStudent -Password[1] : String +GradeLevel[1] : Integer = 1 #Grades[0..*] : Integer +/GPA[1] : Double = Null

CurrentStudent : Student
Name : String = Zachary Password : String = zachrocks GradeLevel : Integer = 1 Grades : Integer = {90, 95, 87, 45, 100, 99} /GPA : Double = 3.44

CRITICAL SKILL

6.6 Learn How to Give Operations with Parameters Detail

Operations can include parameter lists and return values. A *parameter list* is a group of variables that are sent along with the call to the operation. For instance, the Teacher class may have an operation called RecordGrade with parameters that would represent the grade and the student who earned the grade. A *return value* is a single variable that is returned to the caller that could represent a success flag or a computed value. If the Student class has an operation called ComputeGPA, the return value would most likely return a value from zero to four.

Parameters are specified within an operation's parentheses, in the form

parameter name : *data type*

with the parameters separated by commas.

In the following example, two parameters are passed to the ChangePassword operation, OldPassword and NewPassword. A return value is also specified by appending " : Boolean" to the end of the operation. Any data type can be used as the return value. In this case, a Boolean value is returned to indicate whether or not the change of the password was successful. Boolean values can be either True or False.

Student
+Name[1] : String = NewStudent -Password[1] : String +GradeLevel[1] : Integer = 1 #Grades[0..*] : Integer +/GPA[1] : Double = Null
+AddGrade(in Grade : Integer = 100) +ClearGrades() +ChangePassword(in OldPassword : String, in NewPassword : String) : Boolean

TIP
You can omit the parameter name in a parameter list as a shorter alternative. The previous example could be written as ChangePassword(in String, in String) : Boolean, but in this example, the fact that the first String is to be used as the old password and the second String is to be used as the new password is not adequately expressed. It is my suggestion that you always give your parameters names.

In addition to providing each parameter name and data type, you can optionally specify a parameter kind clause of in, out, or inout. In is the default parameter clause (as shown in the previous illustration). Parameters that are to be passed by value should use the in parameter clause—or not have a parameter clause at all. Passing a parameter by value means that a copy of the data is sent to the operation so that the operation cannot change the main copy of that value.

If you want an operation to modify the main copy of a parameter value that is passed into an operation, you will want to mark that parameter with a parameter kind clause of inout, which means that the value will be passed by reference and that any changes to the value within the operation will affect the main copy of that variable that was used prior to the call to the operation.

The last parameter kind clause is out, which is used when a value is not passed into an operation, but rather the operation returns a value within the parameter itself. This is useful in situations such

Ask the Expert

Q: What kind of values do the data types contain?

A: Depending upon the data type, the values that can be inserted into them are different. For instance, we already said that a Boolean can contain only a True or False value. A Byte can only accept a value from 0–255, which represents eight bits of data, or a byte. The following table lists the other common data types and the type of data they can contain:

Currency	A monetary value
Date	A date and time value
Double, Integer, Long, and Single	Numeric values
Object	A reference to any class instance
String	A text value
Variant	Just about anything; it is a wildcard

as error handling. An operation may be defined with the following structure, RetrieveDataByKey (in Key : String, out ErrorCode : Long) : String. In this example, a Key value is passed to RetrieveDataByKey to ultimately return a String value based upon that Key, but if there is an error, the ErrorCode parameter can contain detailed information regarding the error.

Progress Check

1. Describe an attribute for the Monster class that indicates the default number of heads for a monster is three.

2. Describe an attribute for the Monster class that allows multiple names.

3. Describe the operation that would specify which child a monster will scare.

---

1. +NumberOfHeads : Integer = 3
2. +Names[1..*] : String
3. +ScareSomebody(ChildToScare : Child) : Boolean ← return success!

Project 6-1 Reading a Class Diagram

In this project, you will interpret the following class diagram by recognizing the UML notation learned so far in this module.

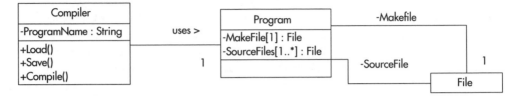

Step by Step

1. Identify the classes that are modeled.

2. Identify all the attributes and their data types that are shown.

3. Identify all the operations shown.

4. Identify the associations found.

5. Identify the roles modeled.

6. Identify the multiplicity used throughout.

Project Summary

As you learned with use case diagrams, you need to feel comfortable understanding and reading class diagrams before you can be expected to model your own. This project should have helped you to identify the different components of the class diagram UML notation that you have learned in this module. For instance, you should have identified that one of the classes modeled was the Compiler class with the Load, Save, and Compile operations.

CRITICAL SKILL
6.7 Learn How to Model a Class Diagram

There are two iterative steps that are involved in creating class diagrams:

1. Finding classes and their associations

2. Finding attributes and operations

It's hard to realize that everything we covered in this module can fit into two steps, but it can, depending upon the level of detail you are going to dive into. Your early class diagrams will be less detailed, but as you iterate through these two steps, and ask more questions of your end users, you will naturally see where more detail is necessary.

A good starting point for class diagrams are your completed use case diagrams that you created in Module 2. In that module, when you were learning how to create use case diagrams, we arrived at the following use case diagram for our grading system.

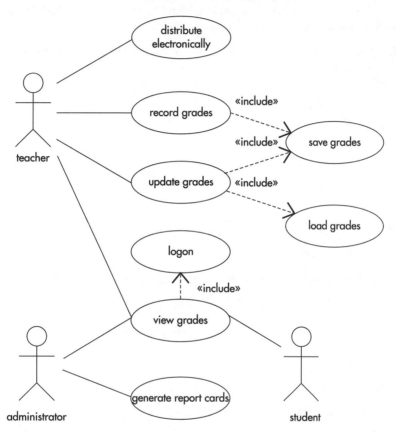

Find Classes and Associations

The first thing you want to do is identify your classes and their associations by analyzing your use case diagram. To find your first batch of classes, identify all of the nouns. In our use case diagram, we find Grades and ReportCard.

Next, you can identify additional classes by also using your actor names. This will also give us Teacher, Student, and Administrator. You should keep in mind that you only want to create a class for an actor if you plan on identifying a piece of information about that actor, such as a name, logon, password, and so forth, or if you will provide functionality for that actor.

TIP

A common technique for GUI development is to wrap the "user" in a class and transfer the actions of the actual user, in the GUI, to the class. For instance, in our case, we may have a screen that allows the user to log on and view grades. In this case, a user of this system would have the operations Logon and ViewGrades that would be the initiation point of the functionality. The user class will in turn call the appropriate related classes to perform this functionality.

At this point, we should review our use cases and make sure they all have a home:

- Distribute Report Cards—Grades Class

- Record Grades—Grades Class

- Update Grades—Grades Class

- Save Grades—Grades Class

- Load Grades—Grades Class

- Logon—?

- View Grades—Grades Class

- Generate Report Cards—ReportCard Class

The first thing we spot is that Logon has no home. Since Logon can also be considered a noun when it is a thing rather than an action, we can add a Logon class to handle the Logon use case.

Now we can begin creating associations for our classes:

- A Teacher distributes the Grades

- A Teacher records the Grades

- A Teacher updates the Grades

- A Grade will save itself

- A Grade will load itself

- A Teacher views Grades

- An Administrator views Grades

- An Administrator generates ReportCards

- A Student views Grades

We can consolidate this list of associations because, in many cases, a class is associated with the same class. In this case, unless the first class plays a different role to the associated classes, they should be consolidated:

- A Teacher maintains Grades
- A Teacher views Grades
- An Administrator views Grades
- An Administrator generates ReportCards
- A Student views Grades

Notice where we have consolidated associations. A Teacher maintains grades by distributing them, recording them, and updating them. We have also left out two use cases:

- A Grade will save itself
- A Grade will load itself

Because, in these two associations, a Grade is associated to a Grade, we can make these associations into private operations within the class so that the class can perform the functionality that it requires.

Next, we want to create classes for any functionality that should have its own class. The ability to identify these classes will come with experience, but I'll tell you that it would be a good idea to pull out the functionality of viewing grades from the Grade class. This can be done because viewing grades is an action that is performed with the use of a Grade class by another class. In this project, we will use a web site, and thus add a WebSite class and its related associations:

- A Logon grants access to a WebSite
- A WebSite displays Grades

Now that we have all of our classes and associations, let's put them into a class diagram.

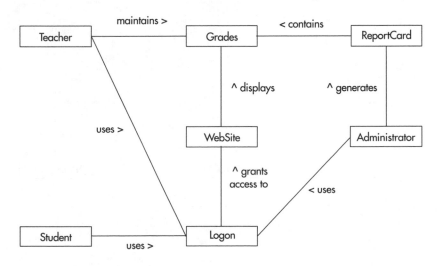

The next step is iterative. We should detail the class diagram some more, perhaps by adding multiplicity, and we should streamline it so that there are no unnecessary classes or associations involved.

In some cases, we will want to identify the multiplicity between the class associations:

- A Teacher maintains at least one Grade
- A Grade is maintained by only one Teacher
- A Grade is contained in only one ReportCard
- A ReportCard contains at least one Grade
- An Administrator generates at least one ReportCard
- A ReportCard is generated by only one Administrator

We can also see that we can consolidate the following three associations:

- A Teacher views Grades
- An Administrator views Grades
- A Student views Grades

We can change our Student class to become an OnlineUser class so that an Administrator and Teacher can also view grades through a web site, which brings us to our next consolidation—the Logon class. The Logon class offers very little functionality; it was added because it didn't belong in the Grades class, but now that we have a separate WebSite class, we can put the functionality in there. You can begin to see how this is an iterative process—it sometimes takes three steps forward and one step backward to make progress.

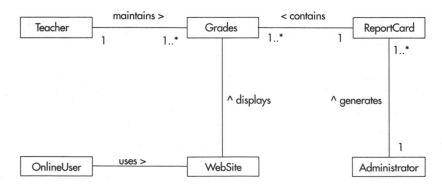

Find Attributes and Operations

Now that we have our classes and associations pretty much in order, we can begin adding attributes and operations to provide the data storage and functionality required to accomplish the use cases in our use case diagram that we are working from.

As you can see in the following illustration, the classes representing the actors are suppressing their attributes and operations. This doesn't mean that they don't exist; it simply means that this class diagram will not go into this detail.

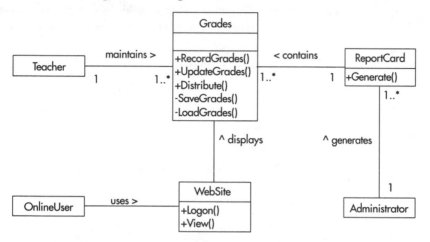

Finally, we want to detail our attributes and operations, and give them parameters, data types, and initial values. This is pretty straightforward and usually is done by somebody close to the development team.

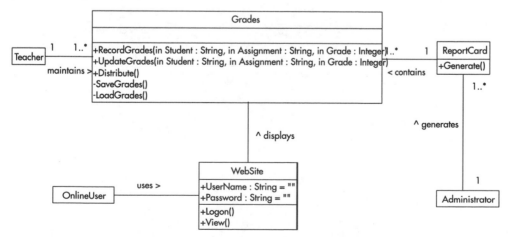

Now that we have our final class diagram, it does not mean that the previous diagrams are not needed. You now have four diagrams that explain how the grading system works. The higher-level diagrams (the ones you created first) are great for enabling management to understand how flow is handled in your system, while the lower-level diagrams (the last one in particular) are excellent for the development team to work with.

Project 6-2 Model a Class Diagram

```
Project6-2_Step2.gif
Project6-2_Step5.gif
Project6-2_Step6.gif
```

In this project, you will model a class diagram from the use case diagram that you modeled in Module 2. You need to follow the steps learned in the previous section of this Module to model a class that will support the use cases in the following use case diagram.

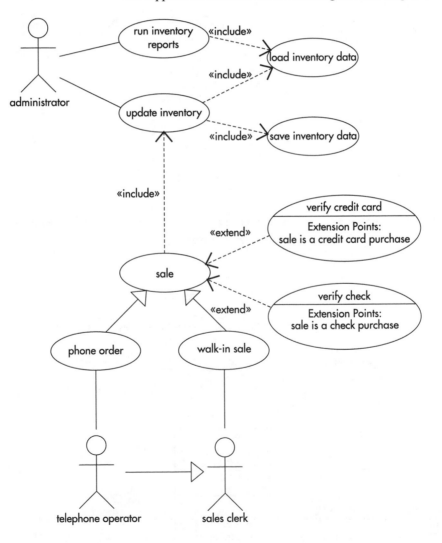

Step by Step

1. Identify the classes that can be found in the use case diagram.

TIP

Remember that you can identify classes by identifying the nouns and actors of the use case diagram.

2. Relate the classes, giving them association names.

NOTE

To assist you in checking your progress on this project, diagrams for selected steps are available online at www.osborne.com. You can easily identify the diagrams available online by referencing the filenames listed with this project's title.

3. Consolidate similar classes.

4. Identify any appropriate role names.

5. Add classes for any independent functionality that is already being encapsulated in another class.

6. Add attributes and operations to provide the functionality required in the class diagram.

7. Detail the operations and attributes giving them data types and parameters.

Project Summary

In this project, you have successfully created a class diagram from a use case diagram. You are quickly on your way to being capable of designing a software product using UML. You should have effectively managed to leverage your knowledge of the basic class diagramming notations. For instance, you should have been able to identify all the classes that can be modeled from the use case diagram, including Telephone Operator and Walk-In Sale. In addition, you should have been able to fully describe your classes by giving them operations with parameter lists, and attributes with data types. If successful, your final class diagram should look similar to that of the one shown next.

(continued)

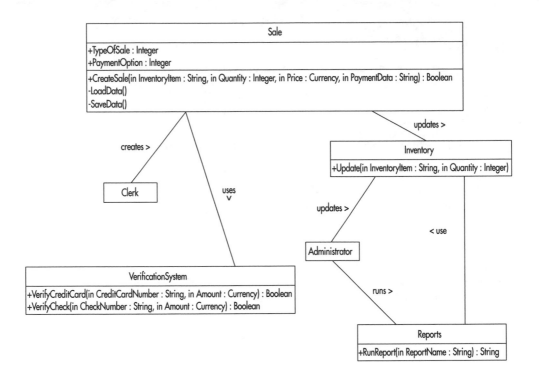

Module 6 Mastery Check

1. Model a class diagram to show the association of a Monster scaring a Child.

2. Add multiplicity to the class diagram you just created to show that a Monster always scares at least one Child, but never more than eight.

3. Show where a child plays the role of a monster to a parent in a class diagram.

4. Give the parent in your class diagram attributes to indicate their age, sex, and name. Default the age to 21.

5. Give the parent in your class diagram an operation that allows it to kiss their monster (returning success/failure).

6. Add a derived attribute to the Parent class called Happy that is true when they successfully kissed their monster.

7. Model an instance of the Parent class, giving it values for its attributes.

8. Modify your class diagram to indicate the package where any classes or objects come from.

9. What are the steps used to create a class diagram?

10. What are the two main components of classes?

Module 7

Collaboration Diagrams

Now that you know how to model class diagrams, we need to take this design to the next level as part of our analysis. The class diagram indicates what classes are part of our system, what they offer, and how they relate, but it does not tell us how they communicate. This is the purpose for which we are going to use the collaboration diagram.

CRITICAL SKILL
7.1 Define Collaboration Diagrams

Collaboration diagrams can be thought of as a cross between class diagrams and sequence diagrams. They actually model objects or roles and their sequenced communication between each other.

As you know from reading previous modules of this book and from creating your own object-oriented designs, classes provide small pieces of isolated functionality to accomplish their individual needs. To build a system, the instances of these classes, the objects, need to communicate and interact with each other. In other words, they need to collaborate.

CRITICAL SKILL
.2 Discover Why We Model Collaboration Diagrams

Collaboration diagrams can be used for a number of reasons, as can most diagrams of UML. Collaboration diagrams are used to model the interactions between objects and roles. They are used to indicate how these objects and roles communicate with each other.

Collaboration diagrams are used to model the interactions between objects and roles, indicating the navigation that is allowed and available across each. Over this navigation, messages can be sent. These messages are the means by which objects communicate and tell other objects or roles what they wish them to accomplish. We model collaboration diagrams to better explain the design as we have analyzed it. We continue modeling for the use cases from our first model to indicate which objects and roles are used to accomplish each task for the user.

CRITICAL SKILL
.3 Identify the Notational Components of a Collaboration Diagram

A collaboration diagram is a collection of objects or roles that interact in a sequence to perform an individual function usually represented earlier in the modeling process as a use case.

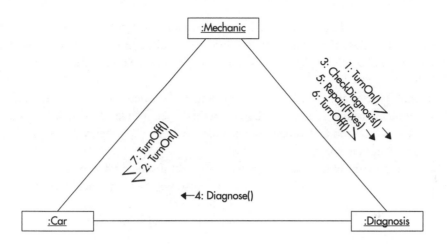

Communication between the objects and roles of a collaboration diagram is done through messages sent along association roles and links that connect them to others.

Objects and Roles

Because a collaboration diagram models system interaction, it must do so with instances of classes that we have designed so far. Since classes do nothing at run time, and their instantiated form (objects) do all the work, it is the interaction between the objects that we are primarily interested in at this point.

There are three types of object instances that we can use in our diagrams.

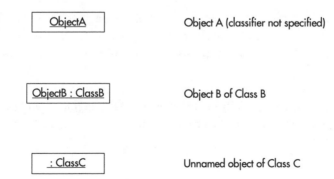

The first type of object instance is the unclassified instance, represented by the first object in the preceding illustration. The name of the unclassified instance is simply underscored as <u>ObjectA</u>. This notation indicates that the class from which this object is instantiated is unknown or unimportant within this particular model.

The second type of object instance is the fully qualified object, which contains a name of the object and its classifier. This notation refers to a specific, unique, named instance. An example would be <u>Zachary : Monster</u>, which indicates that the object, Zachary, is an instance of the Monster class.

The third type of object instance is the unnamed, classified instance. The third and last notation in the preceding illustration shows that this object is named as simply the class name preceded by a colon and underlined. An example would be <u>: Teacher</u>, which represents a generic object instance of the Teacher class.

In addition to object instances, we can show object instance roles in our collaboration diagrams. There are four ways in which we can illustrate object instance roles.

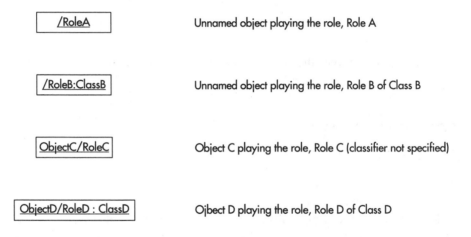

/RoleA	Unnamed object playing the role, Role A
/RoleB:ClassB	Unnamed object playing the role, Role B of Class B
ObjectC/RoleC	Object C playing the role, Role C (classifier not specified)
ObjectD/RoleD : ClassD	Ojbect D playing the role, Role D of Class D

The first notation shown is an unnamed object playing a role. The second notation is an unnamed object playing a role of a specified class. Notice that these two notations indicate to us that you can use either objects that specify their classifier or objects that do not specify their classifier.

The last two notations for object instance roles relate directly to the first two, but the object is named. For instance, a fully qualified object instance role could be <u>Jason/LeadAuthor : Writer</u>, which would indicate that the object, Jason, is an instantiated Writer class, playing the role of LeadAuthor.

Class roles can be used in our diagrams, as well. In this case, we illustrate them without the underlining. There are three choices of notation for specifying class roles.

| /RoleA | Role A |

| :ClassB | Unnamed role of Class B |

| /RoleC : ClassC | Role C of Class C |

The first choice is simply a role name that does not indicate the class that it represents. We know, however, that a role is of a class because it is not underlined, as shown in the first class in the preceding illustration (as compared to the first object, /RoleA, in the previous illustration). You can use the exact opposite in your collaboration diagram, the unnamed role with a classifier. You can also use a fully qualified class role by specifying both the role name and the class name.

Progress Check

1. What are the three notations for object instances in collaboration diagrams?

2. What are the four notations for object instance roles in collaboration diagrams?

3. What are the three notations for class roles in collaboration diagrams?

---

1. Object name without a class name; object and class names; class name without an object name

2. Role name without an object name; role and class names; object and role name without a class name and object; role and class names

3. Role name without a class name; class name without a role name; role and class name

Association Roles

Associations can be carried from the class diagram into the collaboration diagram in the form of *association roles,* which link two class roles. In the following notational example, ClassA plays the role RoleB to ClassB as ClassB plays the role RoleA to ClassA.

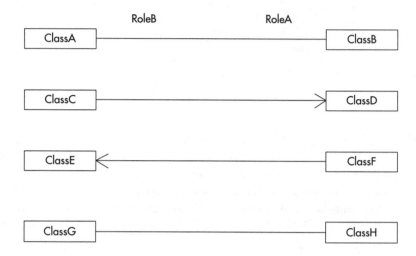

In addition, as shown here, association roles can indicate navigation. They can, by means of an open arrow, indicate in which direction messages flow from one class role to another.

Multiplicity can also be added to the association role to indicate how many objects of one class relate to one object of another class. The following example indicates that the class Project has one source file class that plays the role of the make file, zero to many source files that play the role of code files, and zero to many source files that play the role of resource files.

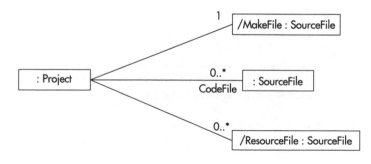

To illustrate navigation, the following example shows that a Department class can communicate with a Teacher class playing the role of a ChairPerson or Staff while being able to communicate with a Student playing the role of an Assistant.

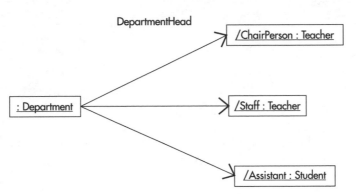

This diagram does not indicate a way in which the Teacher roles nor the Student role can communicate with the Department class. Communication has to originate from the Department class.

Links

Links are used to relate objects in a collaboration diagram. They can represent an instance of an association from a class diagram. A link can be stereotyped with either «parameter» or «local». The «parameter» stereotype indicates that one object is a parameter of the other, while the «local» stereotype indicates that one object has local scope, as a variable, within the other object. This would indicate that the relationship and the variable object are only temporary and will be destroyed along with the owner object.

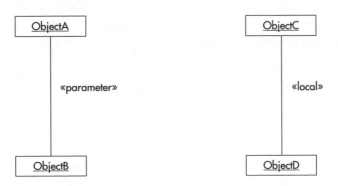

The following illustration shows how links can be used to depict relationships between objects.

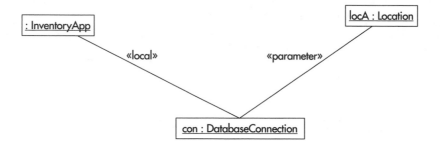

In this example, the InventoryApp has a local variable, con (a DatabaseConnection class instance), which accepts a parameter, locA (a Location class instance).

Progress Check

1. What are association roles?

2. What are links?

3. What are the valid stereotypes for a link in a collaboration diagram?

Messages

Messages are a means for objects to communicate with other objects or for class roles to communicate with other class roles within a collaboration diagram. A message is shown in a collaboration diagram as a text string along a link or association role, with an arrow showing the direction in which the message is traveling along the relationship.

1. A relationship between two classes' roles
2. A relationship between two objects
3. «parameter» and «local»

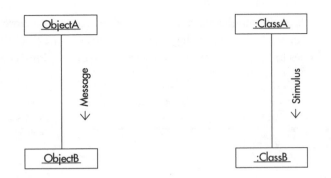

A message can take the form of a class operation, in which it can pass parameters as variables or values. The following example shows how the unnamed Teacher object passes the message, AssignGrade, to the unnamed Student object along with the parameters Class, Assignment, and Grade.

CRITICAL SKILL
7.4 Understand Different Types of Messages

The following are the three types of messages in a collaboration diagram, which are identical to the messages introduced with the sequence diagramming of Module 5:

- **Synchronous messages**   Used when communicating in steps, by completing one step before continuing to the next

- **Asynchronous messages**   Used when you want to communicate in parallel processes

- **Flat messages**   Indicate that the type of message is unknown or unimportant to the model

Synchronous

The type of message that is used in a collaboration diagram is indicated by the type of arrow that is drawn along the association role or link with the message text. A solid arrow indicates that the message is synchronous and that its completion will be necessary before process flow will continue to the next message. The following example shows that the Compiler object sends the message of Load(File) to the FileSystem object synchronously, awaiting completion before continuing.

Asynchronous

Asynchronous messages, as you may recall, indicate that processes can continue without the completion or the delivery of the message. Asynchronous messages are modeled as half of an open arrow next to the message text that is being sent.

In the following example, the Compiler object sends an asynchronous message, Link(ProgramName, Options), to the Linker object. The Compiler will not wait for the Linker to link the program; instead, it will continue on with its work while the Linker is busy linking. In this model, both the Compiler and Linker objects have a thick border around their notation. This indicates that each belongs in its own process and operates independently of the other object.

Flat

A flat message type is diagrammed with an open arrow along the message text and indicates that the message type is unknown or unimportant for the current diagram. In the following model, the two messages coming from the User object are both flat and invoke two different dialog objects by passing the PressButton message. This collaboration diagram shows that we do not know whether the user will send the PressButton message to DialogTwo before, after, or during the message that is being sent to DialogOne.

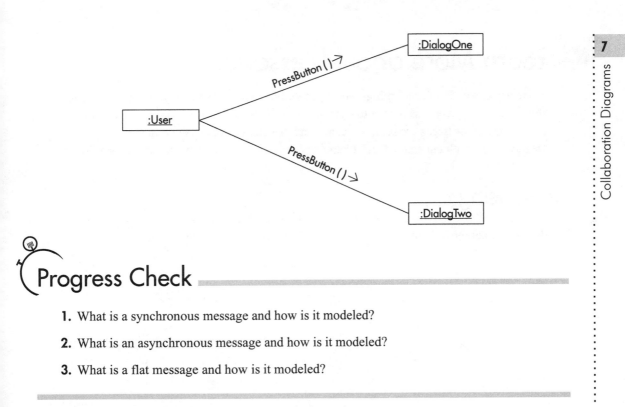

Progress Check

1. What is a synchronous message and how is it modeled?

2. What is an asynchronous message and how is it modeled?

3. What is a flat message and how is it modeled?

---

1. A synchronous message is one that operates in sequence, completing its task before allowing another to continue. It is modeled as a closed arrow next to a message in a collaboration diagram relationship.

2. An asynchronous message is one that operates in parallel with others, not waiting for the completion of its task before allowing another to begin. It is modeled as half an open arrow next to a message in a collaboration diagram relationship.

3. A flat message is one that does not indicate whether the message is synchronous or asynchronous. A flat message is diagrammed as an open arrow next to a message in a collaboration diagram relationship.

Learn More about Messages

There are a number of other things we can do with messages. We can enumerate messages so that they are given a sequence to execute. We can include guard conditions so that we can restrict which messages are sent. We can create instances of objects with messages, just as we have done with our sequence diagrams in Module 5, and we can use messages to iterate.

Sequencing

To sequence messages, we simply need to prefix them with a sequence ID. The easiest way to do this is to number them in the order in which we want them to execute.

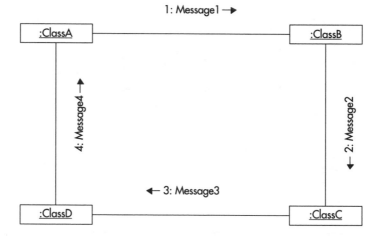

In this example, notice the following sequence of communications:

- ObjectA sends Message1 to ObjectB.

- ObjectB sends Message2 to ObjectC.

- ObjectC sends Message3 to ObjectD.

- ObjectD sends Message4 to ObjectA.

More than one message can accompany a single association role or link. When this occurs, we simply load them on top of each other as in the following example.

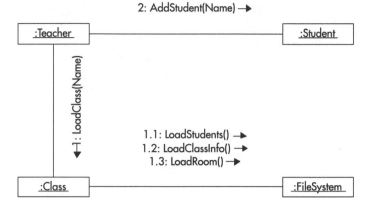

Not only do we show three messages from the Class object to the FileSystem object, we number them differently from the rest. Here we use revision numbers. The order of the sequences in this collaboration diagram is just as you would expect it: 1, 1.1, 1.2, 1.3, 2:

- 1 The Teacher object sends the LoadClass(Name) message to the Class object.

- 1.1 The Class object sends the LoadStudents( ) message to the FileSystem object.

- 1.2 The Class object sends the LoadClassInfo( ) message to the FileSystem object.

- 1.3 The Class object sends the LoadRoom( ) message to the FileSystem object.

- 2 The Teacher object sends the AddStudent(Name) message to the Student object.

Guard Conditions

Guard conditions are used to restrict a message from being sent based upon the evaluation of an expression that "guards" the message. Guards are included in the message between the sequence ID and the message text.

The following notation indicates that from ObjectA, either message 1a, message 1b, or no message at all will be sent based upon the guard conditions. If GuardA evaluates to True, then ObjectA will send the Operation1 message to ObjectB. If GuardB evaluates to True, then ObjectA will send the Operation2 message to ObjectC. If neither GuardA nor GuardB evaluates to True, neither message will be sent.

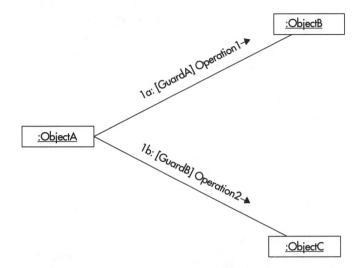

The following example shows how guards and sequencing can be used to indicate an alternative path for an error condition.

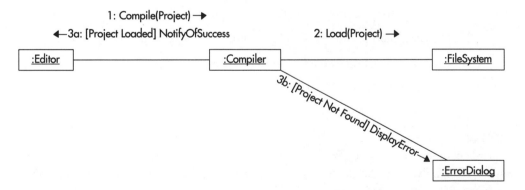

After the Editor tells the Compiler to compile a project, the Compiler tells the FileSystem to load the project. If the project is loaded, a guard condition allows the Compiler to notify the Editor that the project loaded successfully. If the project had trouble loading, then the DisplayError message is sent from the Compiler to an ErrorDialog.

Creating Instances

Just as we saw within sequence diagrams, messages can be used to create instances of objects within a collaboration diagram. In order to do this, a message (usually a constructor or initialize operation) is sent to the newly created object instance. The object is stereotyped with «new» and the message is stereotyped with «create» to reinforce to the reader that the object is actually being created on-the-fly.

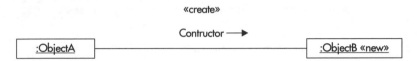

A simple example illustrates how the GradingSystem object can create a Student object with a call of the CreateStudent( ) operation.

In this example, the stereotype «create» is used on the link between the GradingSystem object and the newly created Student object; however, this notation does not need to be used to indicate instantiation of objects. If the message sent is intuitive enough to indicate that the receiving object is being created, the stereotype is not needed.

Iteration

Iteration is a very fundamental and important type of control flow to any system or component. Iteration can easily be modeled in collaboration diagrams and should be used to indicate repeating processes.

There are two notations for iteration in UML. The first notation is used when a single object is sending a message to a group or a collection of other objects. In this notation, we see something a bit new. ObjectB is shown as the name of the object that is represented by more than one box. This actually represents a collection of objects whose count is identified by the multiplicity. In this example, the multiplicity can be any number, indicated by the asterisk by the link between ObjectA and ObjectB.

The asterisk plays an important role in this notation. The asterisk is used as the sequence ID; 1.*: Message indicates that for each ObjectB, Message1 will be sent from ObjectA to the corresponding ObjectB.

The second, similar notation for iteration in UML indicates that a message is sent multiple times from one object to another, as in the following notation.

Here, we see that the Message is being sent from ObjectA to ObjectB five times.

The following example of iteration models the calculation of a GPA for a Student who is linked to a collection of Grades.

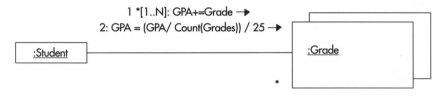

The first sequenced message in this example loops through each Grade object in the collection and accumulates the values. The second sequenced message calculates the average of the total grades by dividing it by the number of grades, and then creates a GPA by dividing that number by 25.

Progress Check

1. If a collaboration diagram contains the following sequence IDs, 1, 3, 4.1, 1.1, 4.1b, 1.1.1, 2, 4.1a, in what order will the messages be sent?

2. What is the stereotype used on the link between objects when a new instance of an object is being created?

3. What is modified in a collaboration diagram to indicate that iteration will occur?

---

1. 1, 1.1, 1.1.1, 2, 3, 4.1, 4.1a, 4.1b
2. «create»
3. The sequence ID

Project 7-1   Reading a Collaboration Diagram

In this project, you will interpret the following collaboration diagram by recognizing the UML notation that you have learned so far in this module. You will also summarize what the collaboration diagram is attempting to model.

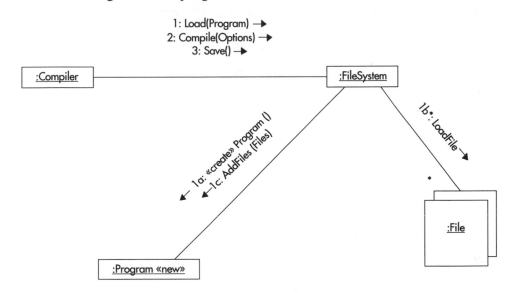

Step by Step

1. Identify the objects.

2. Identify the sequence of events.

3. Summarize the intent of the collaboration diagram.

Project Summary

Congratulations! You have successfully analyzed your first collaboration diagram by leveraging your knowledge of UML, links, messages, and sequencing. If you understood the collaboration diagram, you would have identified that this collaboration diagram models a compiler loading all the files belonging to a program, compiling them, and saving the output.

The next section of this module prepares you to model your own collaboration diagrams to better elaborate your system model.

Learn How to Model Collaboration Diagrams

There are basically three steps to modeling collaboration diagrams:

1. Identify the elements that belong in your diagram.

2. Model the structural relationships between these elements.

3. Model the instance level diagram.

For this section of the module, we are going to model a collaboration diagram for our grading system. The particular use case we are going to model is a Teacher using the Website to log on and check a student's grades.

Identify the Elements of the Diagram

First, we need to identify what elements, or classes, are going to be involved in our collaboration diagram. From the use case that is described to us, we can identify that we definitely need Teacher, Student, and Grade classes, but the rest of the classes may not be so evident to us.

To provide the functionality that the use case requires, we need more classes than these three classes. How is the Teacher class going to interact with the Student class? Where is the Student class going to get its data? How is the Teacher going to log on? By asking ourselves these questions and others, we begin to realize that we need more classes to achieve our goal. In these situations, we need to use helper or utility classes provided for this very reason.

For our grading system, we need a Website class that will provide the location from which the interaction will take place. We also need a Database class that will provide the functionality to retrieve information for the student. Finally, we need a Security class that will provide the means for the Teacher to log on.

As you can see from our selected elements (classes), we can group them into categories based upon function. We have our original elements, or domain classes, our control classes (used to coordinate functionality between the domain classes), and our interface class, the Website.

Model the Structural Relationships

The next step is to identify the relationships between these classes. During this step, we begin to model an early stage of the collaboration diagram as we add links and association roles between the class roles.

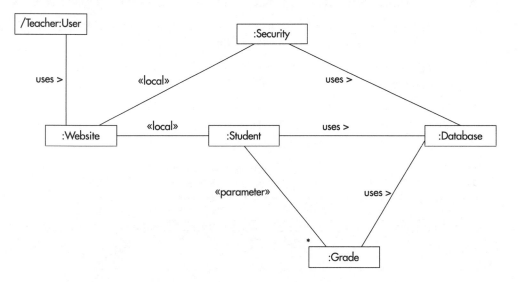

In this diagram, we have changed the :Teacher class into /Teacher:User, which is a User class playing the role of a Teacher. We can anticipate using User again elsewhere, with similar functionality, so we look to separate it into its own class.

In the preceding diagram, we see that the User uses the Website (the interface class), the Website includes local copies of the domain and control classes (Security, Student, and Grade), and the Database class is used by the control classes. Because the Database class has no indication that it is «local», we can assume that it is global and shared by all instances of the classes in this diagram.

Model an Instance-Level Diagram

The final step of modeling our collaboration diagram involves turning the diagram we have modeled thus far into an instance-level diagram (see Figure 7-1). This means that we need to change our class roles into object instances and specify a sequence of messages to perform our use case. This may involve any of the notation that you learned in this module to clarify the messages of the links between the objects, including guards, iteration, instance creation, and the specification of specific message types.

From our final diagram, we can determine that the communication sequence is as follows:

- 1   The User object, playing the role of Teacher, sends the Login(UID, PWD) message to the Website object.

- 1.1   The Website object sends the Validate(UID, PWD) message to the Security object.

- 1.2   The Security object sends the Lookup(UID, PWD) message to the Database object.

- 1.2a   The Security object sends the DisplayMenu( ) message to the Website object if the previous Lookup message resulted in a Pass value.

- 1.2b   The Security object sends the Logout( ) message to the Website object if the previous Lookup message resulted in a Fail value.

- 2   If the menu is displayed (and thus the user is logged in), the User object sends the LoadStudent(Name) message to the Website object.

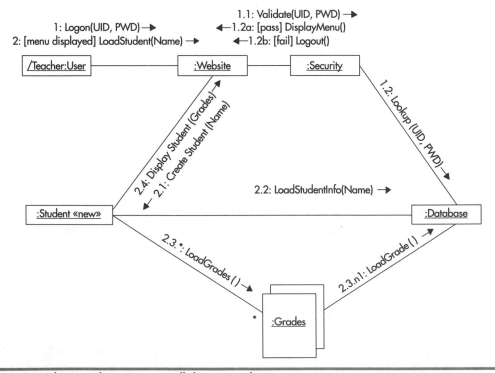

Figure 7-1 The Grading System collaboration diagram

- 2.1   The Website object sends the CreateStudent(Name) message to the Student object to create it.

- 2.2   The Student object sends the LoadStudentInfo(Name) message to the Database object.

- 2.3.*   The Student object sends the LoadGrades( ) message to each of the Grade objects within the Grades collection.

- 2.3.n.1   Each Grade object sends the LoadGrade( ) message to the Database object.

- 2.4   The Student object sends the DisplayStudent(Grades) message to the Website object.

It is a good point to note that, other than checking for the success of logging in the user, this collaboration diagram does not perform any error checking. A more thorough diagram should handle error cases where the student isn't found, the student has no grades, or a database connectivity error occurs.

Project 7-2 Model a Collaboration Diagram

```
Project7-2_Step3.gif
Project7-2_Step4.gif
```

In this project, you will model a collaboration diagram that represents the design for the use case of a Clerk making a credit card sale. In order to do this, you will follow the steps identified in the previous section of this module.

Step by Step

1. Identify the domain class(es).

2. Identify the control class(es).

3. Identify the interface class(es).

NOTE

To assist you in checking your progress on this project, diagrams for selected steps are available online at www.osborne.com. You can easily identify the diagrams available online by referencing the filenames listed with this project's title.

4. Model the structural relationships.

5. Model the instance-level diagram.

(continued)

Project Summary

You have successfully created a collaboration diagram from a use case using analysis and design that has been building up throughout this book. You should have specified messages with a sequence and clarified them with guards and instance creation. If completed successfully, your final collaboration diagram should look like Figure 7-2.

In the next module, you will learn more about class diagrams as you continue learning how to design your systems.

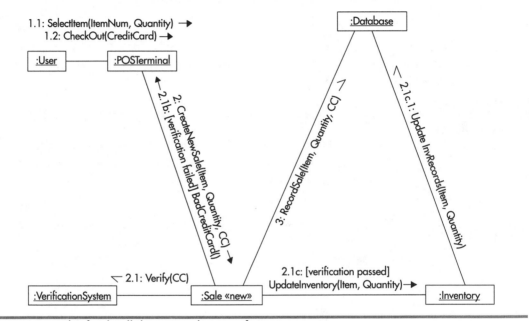

Figure 7-2 The final collaboration diagram for Project 7-2

Module 7 Mastery Check

1. Why do we model a collaboration diagram?

2. What is the difference between association roles and links?

3. What are the three types of messages and what is each used for?

4. Model a collaboration diagram to illustrate the communication for dialing a telephone.

5. What would be some guard conditions for attempting to send an e-mail message?

6. How do you model instance creation in a collaboration diagram?

7. Put the following sequence IDs in order:
   1, 1.1, 1.1.1, 1.1.2.1, 1.2.1.2, 1.1.2.2, 1.2.1.1, 1.2.2.2, 1.1.1.1, 1.1.2, 1.2, 1.2.2

8. What is the notation for an object named Kong, of class Server, playing the role of a WebServer?

9. What are the steps required to create a collaboration diagram?

10. What are the valid stereotypes for a link in a collaboration diagram?

Module 8

Further Explanation of Class Diagrams

There is much more to learn about classes—much more than what this book is going to cover. This module will fully equip you with the remainder of the basic notation and techniques so that you can continue on with your UML learning experience. This module discusses two other specific forms of association relationships, aggregation and composition. It illustrates how to use these two notations to show that classes consist of other classes. It also shows you how to use association annotations and end notations so that you can better describe your association relationships.

Learn about Aggregation and Composition Associations

In previous modules, we've taken a look at associations between classes, and you have learned that they are represented in a class diagram with a single line connecting the two classes. In this section, we take a look at how you can better qualify these associations by classifying and diagramming them as either aggregations or compositions. Both of these new types of associations depict what we call *whole-part* relationships, where one whole class is made up of, or consists of, other classes.

Aggregation

Aggregation is used to illustrate the whole-part relationship between two classes where one class is considered a whole, made up of one or more classes comprising its parts. In an aggregation, the part classes can exist without the whole, but when they are aggregated to a whole, they are used to comprise that class.

An aggregation is represented with the normal association line, but with an empty diamond at the class representing the whole.

As an example, a CPU and a display can both be classes that would exist on their own just fine, but when they are associated to the Computer class, they are parts that make up the whole computer.

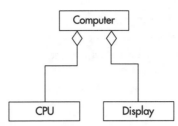

We can extend this example by further isolating the parts of a computer, including a keyboard, mouse, and speakers.

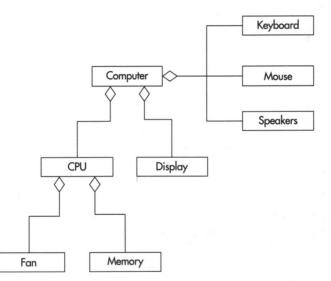

The CPU class, while part of the computer, becomes a whole class itself, as it is made up of the individual parts, fan and memory. Both of these classes, in turn, can exist on their own as well. The previous example also illustrates a different notation for drawing aggregation associations. Notice that keyboard, mouse, and speakers all share the same end point when the aggregation association is connected to the computer. This notation is equivalent to having three individual aggregation associations connect to the computer separately. It is done simply for readability.

TIP

To determine the parts of a whole class, ask yourself these questions: What makes up this class? What pieces, when put together, form this class? A *whole class* is made up of what *part classes*? Be sure to remember the major qualification of aggregation classes—the part classes must be able to exist on their own, within the system that you are modeling.

Because the part classes of an aggregation association can exist on their own, this type of association implies that when the whole class is destroyed, the part classes will still exist. If the part classes are destroyed, the whole class will continue to exist.

Progress Check

1. What do aggregation and composition associations depict?

2. What is aggregation?

3. How is aggregation modeled?

Composition

The second type of association is *composition*, a form of aggregation association in which the part classes used to make up the whole class cannot exist on their own. A composition association is an association relationship between two classes where the whole class is made up of the part classes, and the part classes need the whole class to exist. This relationship implies that the destruction of the whole class means the destruction of the part classes.

The composition association is diagrammed with the single-line association, previously discussed, with the addition of a solid diamond at the whole class end of the line.

Because a composition association indicates that the part classes are mandatory, multiplicity of at least one is always implied for the whole class, as indicated by the 1 in the illustration.

---

1. Whole-part class relationships
2. An association where a whole is made up of parts, but the parts can exist without the whole
3. With an association line and an empty diamond at the whole class

In the following example, a whole database class consists of both tables and queries. These associations are diagrammed with composition, because without the database, neither the tables nor the queries would exist.

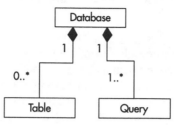

Composition association, like aggregation association, can also be nested, as shown in the following example.

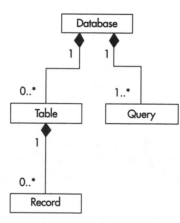

Here, we have added the Record class as a part of the whole Table class. This diagram shows us that zero or more records make up a table. A record cannot exist without a table.

TIP

To determine the parts of a whole class in a composition association, ask yourself these questions: What are the pieces of this class? What pieces are required to form this class? A *whole class* consists of what *part classes*? Be sure to remember the major qualification of composition classes—the part classes cannot exist on their own, within the system that you are modeling.

Ask the Expert

Q: How can I determine what kind of association I need in my diagram?

A: The key difference between aggregation and composition association is whether or not the part classes require the whole class to exist for *them* to exist. This may vary depending upon the system or problem domain that you are modeling. For instance, if you are modeling a database system, as the previous examples were implying, your database may have User classes associated to the Database class. This would most likely be a composition class, because the scope of the project requires that a User be assigned to a Database. If however, we were modeling an entire operating system, where a Database was only one of the classes being modeled, the User class would not have to be tied to the database; in fact, it would probably have a composition association with the operating system, while it would have an aggregation association with the database.

Notice that all the composition association examples in this section show that the part classes have at least a 1 multiplicity to the whole class. This means that the part class has to have at least one whole class, or, the part class cannot exist without the whole.

Composition Using Graphical Containment

An alternative method of modeling composition is called *graphical containment*. With this method, the whole class is drawn as a large box, and all the classes that are part classes are contained inside of this box.

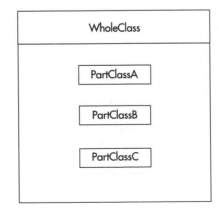

The preceding notation shows three part classes, one whole class, and their composition association with each other. The part classes can easily associate to each other by drawing association lines within the containment class, or they can be associated to classes outside the containment class.

The following example of graphical containment revisits our Database whole class model. In this example, the two part classes, Table and Query, are contained within the Database whole containment class. The multiplicity is specified for this notation inside the part class title box, in the upper-right corner. In this example, the Database class has a 1 to 0..* relationship with the Table class and a 1 to 0..* relationship with the Query class.

```
┌─────────────────────────────────────┐
│              Database                │
├─────────────────────────────────────┤
│                                      │
│                                      │
│      ┌──────────────────────┐        │
│      │ Table        0..*     │        │
│      └──────────────────────┘        │
│                                      │
│      ┌──────────────────────┐        │
│      │ Query        0..*     │        │
│      └──────────────────────┘        │
│                                      │
│                                      │
└─────────────────────────────────────┘
```

Progress Check

1. What is composition?

2. What are the two ways to model composition?

3. What is the difference between composition and aggregation?

---

1. An association where a whole is made up of parts, but the parts cannot exist without the whole

2. With an association line and an empty diamond at the whole class, or with the whole class as a large box with the part classes modeled within it

3. Aggregation part classes can exist without the whole class, whereas composition part classes cannot exist without the whole class

Using Aggregation and Composition with Generalization

Aggregation and composition associations are class relationships that can be combined with generalization to further extend our models, as shown in the next example.

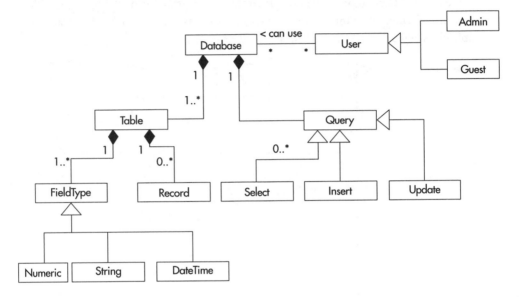

Here we see the use of both aggregation and composition associations with the same classes. For instance, Numeric, String, and DateTime are all types of FieldType, which is a part of the whole class Table.

Project 8-1 Modeling Aggregation and Composition

```
Project8-1_Step1.gif
Project8-1_Step2.gif
Project8-1_Step3.gif
Project8-1_Step4.gif
```

In this project, you will create a class diagram using all the types of relationships that you have learned so far in this book, including ordinary associations, generalizations, aggregations, and composition. You will apply your knowledge of how to construct a class diagram from requirements.

The following is a list of the requirements for an inventory system that will be used by a manufacturing and repair plant. Construct a class diagram from this information.

● Inventory consists of two things—parts and products. All parts and products are always in inventory if they are in the system.

● Products are made up or two of more parts, and the system can hold an unlimited number of parts and products.

● Some of the parts that are in the inventory include flywheels, cogs, and afterburners.

● An inventory clerk maintains the inventory. An assembler builds the products and a repairman repairs them.

● A finished product can have up to three stickers (and it always has to have at least one): Manufacturer stickers indicate that the product has been built; Repair stickers indicate that the product has been repaired; and FCC stickers indicate that the product includes an afterburner (they interfere with radio waves, I guess…).

Step by Step

1. Evaluate the first requirement and include composition association.

NOTE

To assist you in checking your progress on this project, diagrams for selected steps are available online at www.osborne.com. You can easily identify the diagrams available online by referencing the filenames listed at the beginning of this project.

2. Evaluate the second requirement and include aggregation relationships and multiplicity.

3. Evaluate the third requirement and include generalized associations.

4. Evaluate the fourth requirement and add the appropriate actors.

5. Evaluate the fifth requirement and include any other associations that are required for it.

(continued)

Project Summary

In this project, you should have successfully modeled a complex class diagram that included generalization and association relationships, over a dozen classes, and multiplicity. If successful, your model should look similar to the following.

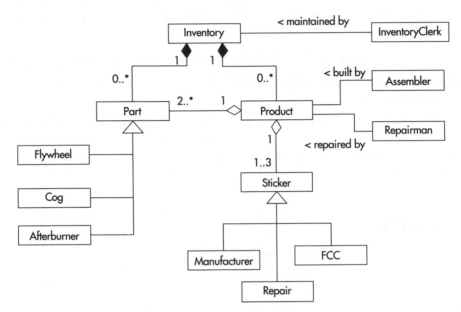

As you can see from actually modeling your own diagrams, this iterative process requires change at every step. By simply looking at the diagrams for each step in the project, we see that classes are moved, associations are joined and broken apart, and lines are rerouted. This is fine and should be done as you add more and more to your diagrams. In the next section, we are going to look at some smaller things that can be done to associations to detail your models even further.

CRITICAL SKILL
8.2 Learn about Association Annotations

Now you are going to learn about associations and how to annotate them with constraints and discriminators. Generalization *constraints* are used to indicate that the generalization has a condition associated with it. *Discriminators* are used to indicate what role a generalization relationship is playing for the two involved classes.

Constraints

Constraints can be predefined or user-defined. User-defined constraints can take on any meaning that you wish them to in the context of your system. Here we are going to learn about some of the predefined constraints that the UML provides us with. You may choose to make up your own constraints that better fit your system and situation after you have learned about these predefined constraints.

There are two ways in which you can model a constraint for a generalization. When you have two or more generalizations that you would like to use the same constraint on, you can draw a dashed line through each of the generalizations and label that line with the constraint name in curly braces ({...}). If you only have one generalization, or if multiple generalizations share the hollow-arrow portion of the association, you can simply model the constraint in curly braces toward the hollow arrow.

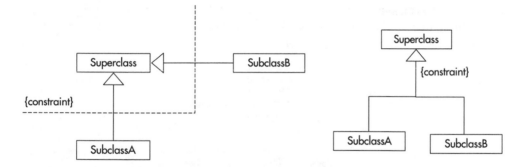

The first constraint we are going to look at is the *incomplete constraint*. This constraint indicates to the reader that the list of generalized, or subclassed, classes is not complete— meaning that the diagram does not show them all. This is sometimes useful to point out to the reader so that they realize there is more than what is in front of them, usually on another diagram.

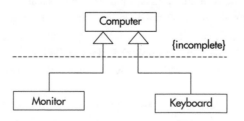

The second type of constraint we are going to see is the *complete constraint*. This constraint is the opposite of the incomplete constraint in that it tells the user that what you see is all there is.

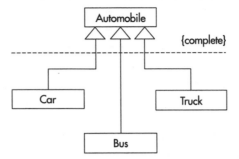

The *disjoint constraint* is a little tougher to understand than the complete and incomplete constraints. The disjoint constraint tells the user that the generalized classes immediately below the constraint cannot be subclassed with common classes. Take a look at the following example to better understand what is involved.

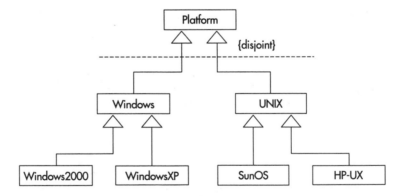

Here, you can see that the root superclass, Platform, has two subclasses, Windows and UNIX. The disjoint constraint says that both the Windows and UNIX classes cannot share further subclasses. The example shows that they each have their own distinct subclasses, but if a generalization was drawn from the WindowsXP class to the UNIX class, this would be invalid because of the disjoint constraint. Windows XP cannot be both a type of Windows and a type of UNIX platform.

The final type of generalization constraint that we will look at in this module is the *overlapping constraint*, which acts as the disjoint constraint's opposite. The overlapping constraint shows to the reader that the two subclassed classes share a common subclass.

In the following example, we see that a Database class has two types, Relational and OLAP, which in turn share a common type, DataWarehouse.

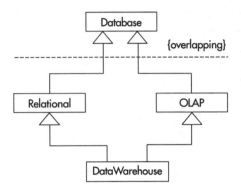

TIP

Remember that it is not mandatory to use any of these constraints. They are meant to be used as a helper to your models, giving them further clarification. If you feel that something is missing or misunderstood in the diagram that you have modeled, consider using a constraint to clarify what you mean.

Progress Check

1. What does the complete constraint indicate?

2. What is the opposite of a disjoint constraint?

3. What does a disjoint constraint indicate?

Discriminators

Discriminators are used to show what a generalization is doing. They indicate to the reader the role of the subclass in the generalization association as it applies to the related superclass. The

---

1. That all the subclasses of a superclass are modeled
2. An overlapping constraint
3. That the subclasses of a superclass cannot have further common subclasses

notation for discriminators is very simple. The discriminator is labeled close to the hollow arrow of the association.

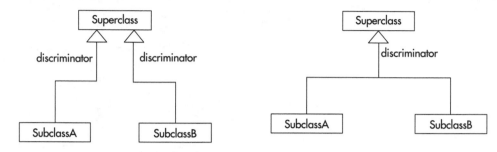

A discriminator cannot be the name of an attribute of the superclass, nor can it be the name of any association relating to the superclass. In the following example, we use the discriminator, type, to indicate that the Flywheel and Afterburner subclasses are types of the Part class.

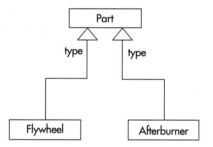

A more detailed example is shown next. This example adds discriminators to a diagram of four classes with an overlapping constraint specified.

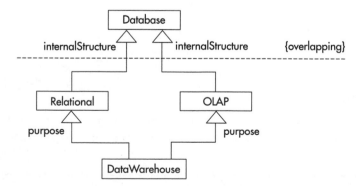

This example reads as "a DataWarehouse is the purpose of a Relational and OLAP structural database."

CRITICAL SKILL
8.3 Understand End Notations

The last thing you are going to learn in this module is how to model an end notation. You are going to learn about ordering, sorting, and navigation for the associations that we have discussed earlier in this module. Ordering and sorting allow you to specify to the reader that subclasses involved in relationships with a superclass have a specific order, while you can use navigation to specify in which direction process flow can travel across association relationships.

Ordering and Sorting

An *ordered constraint* is used to indicate that the objects of one class are related to the object of the other class in a particular order. The order is not specified with this notation. The *sorted constraint* indicates that the objects of the class are sorted when related to the other object of the other class in the association. You can add an ordering constraint or a sort constraint to the bottom portion of any relationship, as shown in the following example.

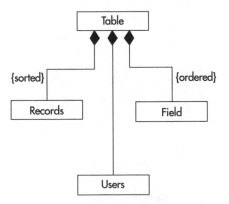

In this example, the Records are sorted in a table, Fields have their own order but Users are not sorted, nor do they have an order.

Navigation

With the associations that we have seen so far, the navigation is generally bidirectional. You can get from one class to another and back through attributes that are exposed to the user in both classes of a relationship. If you don't want your system, or specific class relationship, to operate in this fashion, you can specify a single direction for the navigation. Navigation is indicated with an open arrow pointing to the class that is being accessed.

In the following example, the Record class has a bidirectional relationship with the Table class. The Table class has a public attribute, Records, which allows navigation to each object of the Record class. The Record class has a private attribute, Table, which allows the Record class to navigate back to the composite class Table. The User class has no way of getting to the Table class, but the Table class uses the private Permissions attribute to get to the User. The same is true for the navigation from the Table class to the TypeOfData class—except that the Fields attribute (used for the navigation) is public.

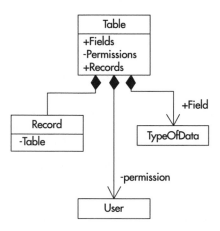

Progress Check

1. What is the purpose of using discriminators?

2. What is the difference between ordered and sorted constraints?

3. How is navigation modeled?

---

1. To indicate the generalization's role
2. Ordering indicates that a specific order is used for a relationship, while sorting indicates that the relationship is sorted
3. With an open arrow at the end of the association in the direction that the navigation will flow

Project 8-2 Modeling More Associations

```
Project8-2_Step1.gif
Project8-2_Step2.gif
Project8-2_Step3.gif
Project8-2_Step4.gif
```

In this project, you will be creating a class diagram using all the types of associations that you have learned so far in this book as well as the association annotations and end notations that you have learned in the second half of this module. You will be applying your knowledge of how to construct a class diagram from requirements.

The following is a list of the requirements for a more detailed look at the Part class from our previous inventory system project. Construct a class diagram from this information.

- Two or more Parts make up a Product, as you learned in the previous project. The Product class can access the Part class, but not the other way around.

- The three types of Parts (Flywheel, Cog, and Afterburner) do not comprise a complete list of the parts in the inventory system—but they are all we care about at this time.

- A Flywheel can have two distinct layouts that do not share any further similarities—a tooth flywheel and a gear flywheel.

- An Afterburner can be classified into either a turbo or a hydro afterburner. Both of these types can be broken down into a ballistic type.

- A ballistic hydro or turbo afterburner is made up of plutonium marbles that have to be arranged just right in order to work.

Step by Step

1. Model the first requirement with whole-part relationships, navigation, and multiplicity.

NOTE

To assist you in checking your progress on this project, diagrams for selected steps are available online at www.osborne.com. You can easily identify the diagrams available online by referencing the filenames listed at the beginning of this project.

2. Model the second requirement and include the appropriate constraints.

3. Model the third requirement using constraints and generalization associations.

(continued)

4. Model the fourth requirement and generalize the Afterburner class.

5. Model the fifth and final requirement using the appropriate associations.

Project Summary

You should have successfully modeled another complex class diagram, but this time you have used far more of UML to enhance the readability for the reader. If successful, your model should look similar to this:

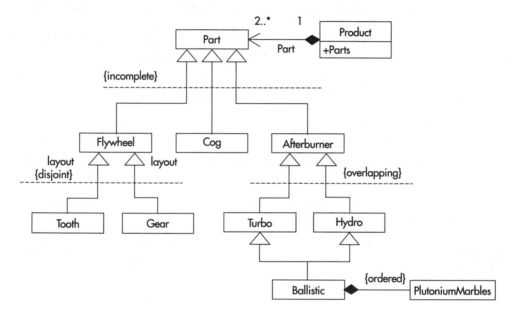

You did it! You learned everything I'm going to teach you about class diagrams. These are not, by far, the last things to learn about class diagramming, but for the beginner, the buck stops here. This will give you the information you need to model your systems. As your needs grow, you can continue looking into UML for more information. But for now, we must move on to another UML diagram.

✓

Module 8 Mastery Check

1. Describe aggregation and composition.

2. Model the associations between a stereo system and its receiver and speakers.

3. Model the components of an e-mail message with associations.

4. Add navigation to the e-mail message model.

5. Model the e-mail application using graphical containment.

6. What are the four types of generalization constraints you learned in this module?

7. What are the types of composition constraints you learned in this module?

8. Model an overlapping constraint using the following classes: File, Binary, Text, WordDocument, and DatabaseFile.

9. What is the difference between a constraint and a discriminator?

10. What are some examples of predefined constraints?

Module 9

Further Explanation
of Sequence
Diagramming

189

n Module 5 of this book, you learned how to use sequence diagrams to illustrate interaction between objects from somewhat of a high-level perspective. In later modules, we built upon those sequence diagrams with class diagrams, moving from analysis models to design models. The sequence diagram, just as the class diagram, can be used to model design as well as analysis.

In this module, you will learn how to model your previous sequence diagrams with more design detail, including how to specify which objects have focus and how to model iteration within your object or group of objects. You also will learn a great deal more about messages that are passed between objects, including how to model messages that take time to execute and how to model parameters and arguments to these messages.

CRITICAL SKILL
9.1 Learn about Control Rectangles

The first things that you add to your sequence diagrams when designing your system are control rectangles, which are used to indicate that an object has control and that it is currently processing some sort of information or that it is waiting for a piece of information. In a sequence diagram, control rectangles are drawn as vertical hollow rectangles over the object's lifeline.

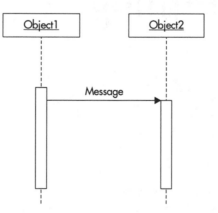

Control rectangles can be modeled as shown in the preceding notation to illustrate general focus of control, or they can be altered to specify activation phases.

Using Control Rectangles

The control rectangle notation is a simple notation that helps the reader understand when an object is involved in a sequence of messages. In most cases, one object has focus at a time; however, in event-driven applications with asynchronous functionality, this is not always the case. Take for instance the following example of a sequence diagram enhanced from Module 5.

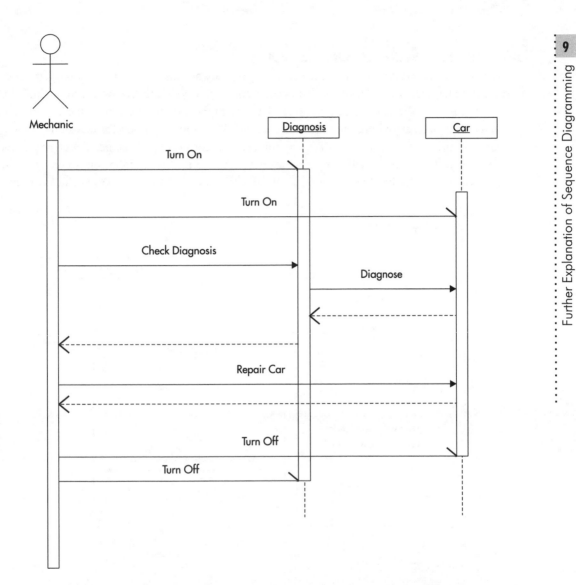

This diagram shows the Mechanic's control rectangle completely obscuring the Mechanic's lifeline. This indicates that the Mechanic is involved for the life of the entire sequence of events modeled in the sequence diagram. The Diagnosis and Car objects, on the other hand, are a different story. These objects are not involved until they are instantiated, or turned on by the Mechanic.

Specifying Activation Periods

Sometimes, objects within a sequence diagram don't always maintain control through the life of the model. Take for instance, the following example of a Web Interface object communicating with a Database Wrapper object. As you saw in one of the previous examples, the Teacher had focus when arriving within the sequence diagram. The proper notation for this situation is shown in the following example. The control rectangle for the object extends directly up to the object box. If a piece of the lifeline were to show between the box and the control rectangle, it would indicate that the object became involved within the operations of the sequence diagram.

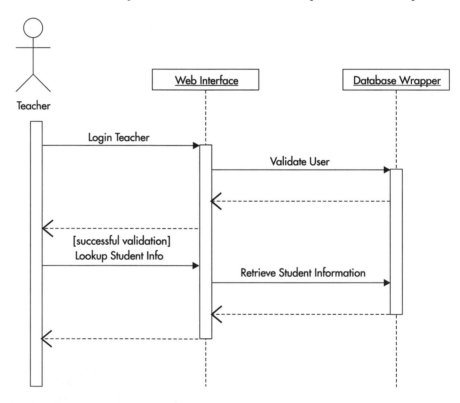

In this example, the Database Wrapper object doesn't necessarily maintain control from the moment the user is validated to the time the student information is retrieved. Each web request made by an instance of the Teacher class may create a new instance of the Database Wrapper class, or it may invoke the Database Wrapper class instance to wake up to process something for it once again.

The control rectangle does not have to extend all the way to the end of an object's lifeline, nor does it have to be continuous, as shown in the following notation.

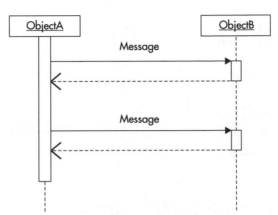

This notation shows how an object can completely lose control when a message has completed. This signifies that the object is not waiting for further instructions.

The following example shows how we can modify the previous Web Interface object to Database Wrapper object sequence diagram to break up the activation.

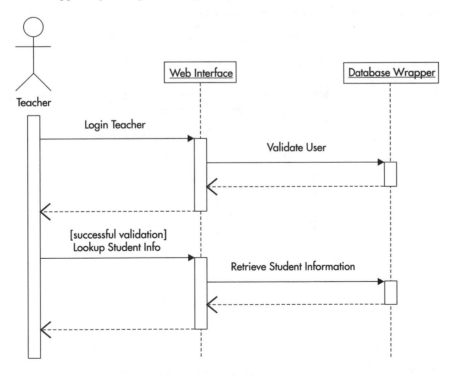

In this example, we also have broken the activation of the Web Interface, which is not activated again until the user has requested another page.

Progress Check

1. What do control rectangles signify?

2. What is activation?

3. What is meant when an object's lifeline is completely obstructed by a control rectangle?

9.2 Learn How to Model Time

Sometimes it may be necessary to indicate that a message from one object to another is not instantaneous. This occasionally occurs when two applications are communicating with each other over the Internet or a network.

To model that a message takes time to complete and execute, the message is drawn on a slight slant in the direction that the message is being sent.

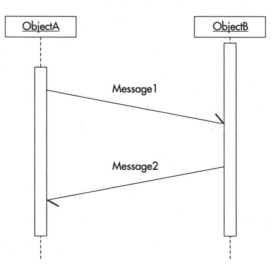

---

1. An object is involved with the sequence of messages during the time that a control rectangle occupies its lifeline
2. The time that an object has focus
3. The object is involved with the entire sequence of messages modeled in the sequence diagram

Not only can you simply say that a message takes time to complete, you can specify constraints to how much time it is allowed to take, or a duration for a group of messages to complete.

Indicating Changes in Time

An example of a situation in which a message may take some time to complete is when you are communicating with an e-mail server. Sometimes e-mail servers are halfway across the world, linked by the Internet, whereas other times they are around the corner, in the next room, connected via the network. Because the e-mail server is an external object, with the potential of consuming time to communicate with, we can model our messages being sent to and from it as taking time.

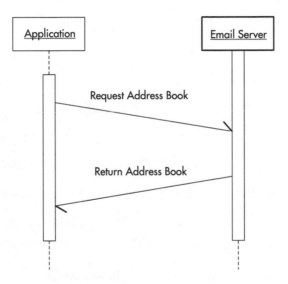

This example shows that our Application sends an asynchronous message requesting a copy of the address book from the Email Server. Because this message is drawn with a slant, it shows that the message may take time to reach the server and to execute. In turn, the return message containing the address book may also take time to execute.

Modeling Time Constraints

We can add constraints to these messages to indicate a time frame in which they need to execute. We certainly do not want to wait three days for a request for an e-mail server's address book, so we can specify a shorter time frame. The notation for a constraint on the time of a message is simply added to a note box and placed in curly braces next to the message that the constraint is applied to.

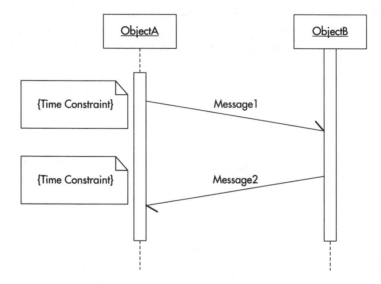

UML has generic constraint functions that can be used, such as sendTime and receiveTime. However, you can make up any functions that you see fit in order to express the system you are designing.

The following example shows that we can use time constraints in a similar asynchronous time-consuming sequence diagram to add constraints for connecting (five seconds maximum) and receiving e-mails (two minutes maximum).

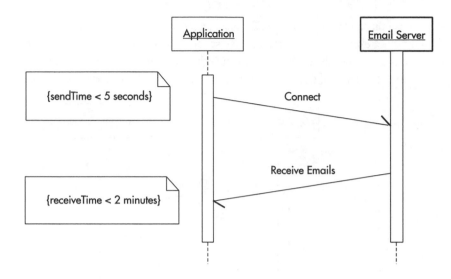

Modeling Time Duration

You can also specify the overall length of time that a group of messages can take to execute time-consuming messages, using the following constraint notation.

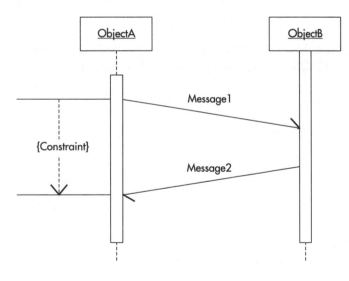

We can use this notation to indicate, for instance, that the total time to connect and retrieve e-mails should not exceed two minutes and five seconds. This notation differs from the preceding notation in that it does not differentiate between taking two minutes to connect and five seconds to receive e-mails and taking five seconds to connect and two minutes to receive e-mails.

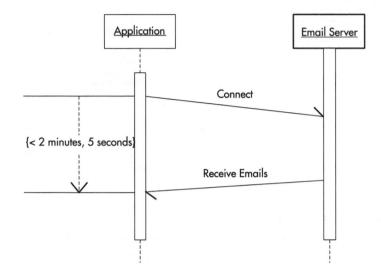

Progress Check

1. How is time modeled in sequence diagrams?

2. What is a time constraint?

3. What is a time duration?

---

1. With a message slanting toward its called object
2. A constraint that indicates the maximum time within which a single message can execute
3. A constraint that indicates the maximum time within which a group of messages can execute

Project 9-1 Reading Sequence Diagrams for Activation and Time

The following diagram contains control rectangles, activation periods, and some timed messages. Step through the diagram, indicating which object has control, and then describe the timed messages modeled.

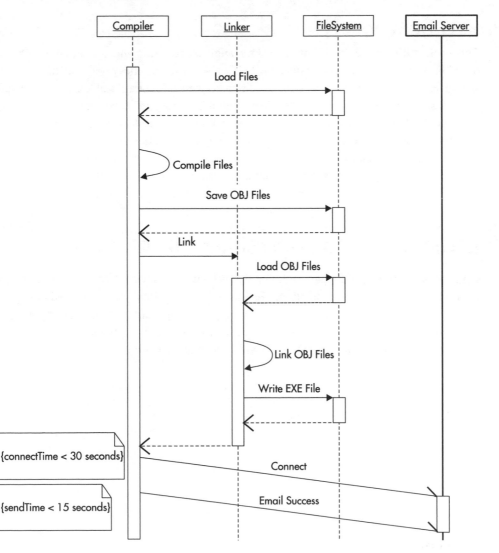

(continued)

Step by Step

For the sequence diagram:

1. Identify the process flow.

2. Identify the timed messages.

Project Summary

This project illustrated the use of control rectangles, activation and activation periods, and timed messages and time constraints. By being able to successfully read this diagram, you should have proven that you understand the difference between control and focus, how activation is used, and how time can be modeled. You should have recognized that the Compiler sends a message, Link, to the Linker, giving it control and focus, as well as the fact that the Compiler has up to 30 seconds to connect to the Email Server asynchronously.

In the next portion of this module, you will learn how to model iteration and truly turn your sequence diagram into a design diagram by specifying more-detailed message calls between objects.

CRITICAL SKILL
9.3 Learn How to Model Iteration

Iteration is a very important part of design that we have not yet covered. Being able to model iteration gives you the ability to design for and while loops. Iteration is modeled in sequence diagrams by encompassing the entire set of iterated message calls with a rectangle and by giving it a guard condition that indicates multiplicity. For example, the following notation illustrates that ObjectA will call ObjectB while the guard condition is true.

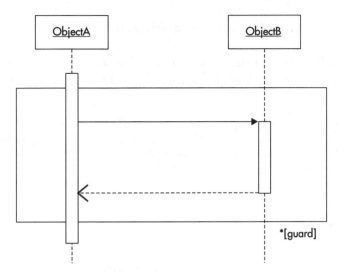

Modeling Loops

The following is a simple example of how iteration is modeled in sequence diagrams to show an application saving all of its dirty files (files that have been changed, but not yet saved).

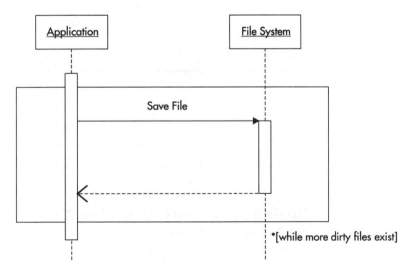

In this example, the iteration of the Save File message will continue while more dirty files exist to save.

You can use the iteration notation to show nested loops by encompassing one iteration within another. The following example shows how an Editor ultimately compiles every project that is open.

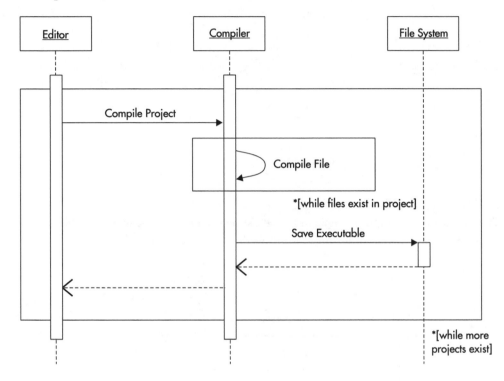

The Editor object is involved in the outer loop used to compile individual projects. While uncompiled projects exist, the loop will continue. Within the loop, the Compiler has its own iteration to compile individual files within the current project.

Note that in this example, not every activation period is specified. Just as with many other notations within UML, you do not always have to specify everything. If it were of importance to you to indicate which object had focus, or if it were not apparent, you could add the solid vertical rectangles to the control rectangles to indicate activation.

Modeling Recursion

Recursion is a type of iteration, but in UML, it is modeled differently. The following is the notation for recursion. Here, another control rectangle is shown as a child of the original with a call from one to the other.

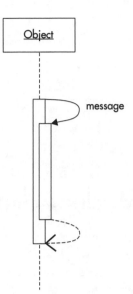

Recursion is used in many places, including sorting. The following example shows a generic view of a sorting design algorithm indicating that items are sorted individually until all the items are sorted.

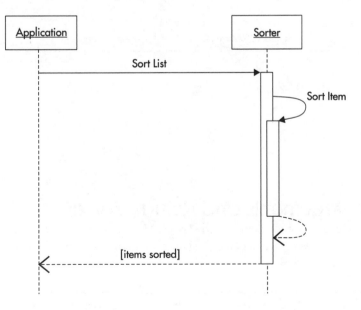

Progress Check

1. How are iterations modeled?

2. What is the role of a guard in an iteration?

3. How is recursion modeled?

CRITICAL SKILL

9.4 Learn How to Model Advanced Messages

Messages in sequence diagrams can contain a number of additional pieces of information other than simply their name. Besides guards, which you have already seen in sequence diagram messages, messages may contain arguments, return values, and sequence expressions.

The message notation is shown in the following illustration as a call from one object to another.

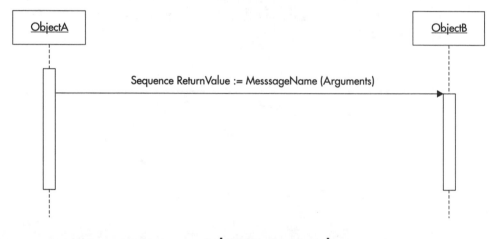

Message Arguments and Return Values

Messages are equivalent to operations in classes. Messages can have a list of arguments that are passed to the called object and they can contain up to one return value that is eventually returned to the calling object.

---

1. With a rectangle surrounding the messages that are part of the iteration and a multiplicity guard at the bottom-right corner of the rectangle

2. The guard is an expression that indicates when the iteration should occur

3. By a child control rectangle as part of the original, and a message call from the original to the child

The following example shows how the message notation of specifying arguments and return values can be used to calculate and return a student's GPA.

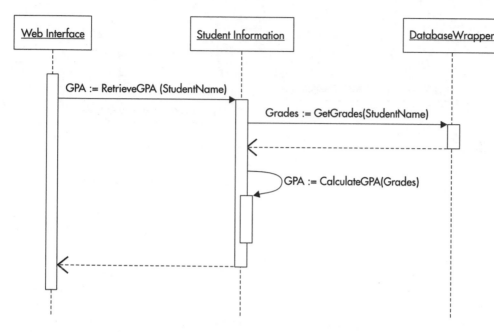

In this example, the Web Interface sends the RetreiveGPA message with the student's name to the Student Information object, which will eventually return a GPA value. This is equivalent to saying that the Web Interface object calls the RetreiveGPA operation of the Student Information object.

From here, the Student Information object calls the GetGrades operation of the Database Wrapper object with the student name, returning the Grades for that student. The GPA is calculated from the Grades as the Student Information object calls its own CalculateGPA operation. The GPA is finally returned in the return message to the original RetrieveGPA call from the Web Interface.

Specifying Message Sequences

You can specify the order of messages in sequence diagrams by preceding any message with a sequence expression. A sequence expression can be a number or any text-based description that makes sense for the ordering. The following example adds sequence expressions to the previous example.

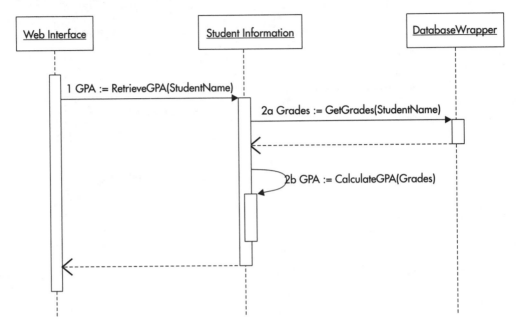

In this updated diagram, you can clearly see that the first message to be sent is the RetrieveGPA message, followed by GetGrades (2a), and then CaclulateGPA (2b).

Other examples of sequence expressions could include:

● 1, 2, 3, 4, 5, 6

● i, ii, iii, iv, v, vi

● 1.1, 1.2, 1.3, 1.4, 1.5, 1.6

● 1.1, 1.1.1, 1.1.1.1, 1.1.1.2, 1.1.2

● first, second, third, fourth, last

CRITICAL SKILL

9.5 Understand How to Add Notes to Sequence Diagrams

Comments can be added to any diagram, including the sequence diagram using the Note notation. The following illustration enhances the previous examples to include iteration so that all students' GPAs are calculated. A note to the left of the iteration explains to the reader, in English, what is happening. Because sequence diagrams can become very cluttered with just the notation of a sequence of events, I suggest using notes to clarify potential areas that can be misunderstood, as a precaution.

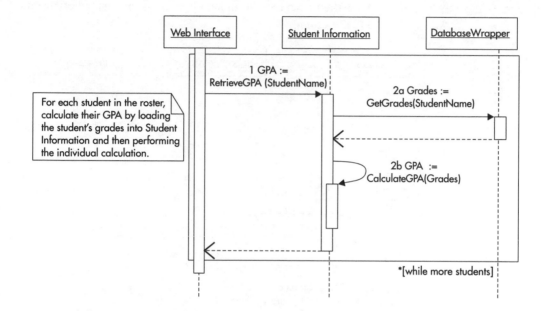

Progress Check

1. What are the additional components of the message notation learned in this module?

2. What is another way of saying Object A sends Message 1 to Object B?

3. How are comments illustrated in a sequence diagram?

1. Arguments, return value, and sequence expression
2. Object A calls the operation, Message 1, of Object B
3. With the Note notation—a box with a folded corner—to the left of the explained portion of the diagram

Project 9-2 Further Sequence Diagram Modeling

Project9-2_Step1.gif
Project9-2_Step2.gif
Project9-2_Step3.gif

The following sequence diagram is the solution to Module 5's Project 5-2. It is an analysis sequence diagram illustrating how an Administrator can remove an item from a system's inventory using the POS System.

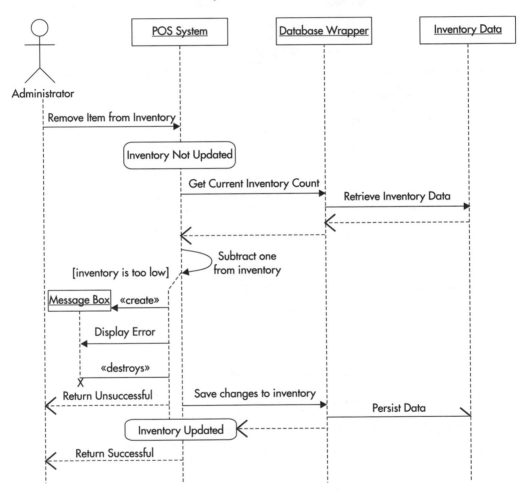

With this diagram, add control rectangles and activation, time and iteration, message clarification, and notes.

Step by Step

1. Model control rectangles and activation.

NOTE

To assist you in checking your progress on this project, diagrams for selected steps are available online at www.osborne.com. You can easily identify the diagrams available online by referencing the filenames listed at the beginning of this project.

2. Model time and iteration.

3. Model message clarifications.

4. Add notes to explain the sequence diagram.

Project Summary

This project should have proven your ability to model sequence diagrams using all of the notation you have learned in this module, including control rectangles, activation, message time consumption, iteration, notes, and object operation calls through the use of advanced message notation. If successful, your diagram should look similar to the following:

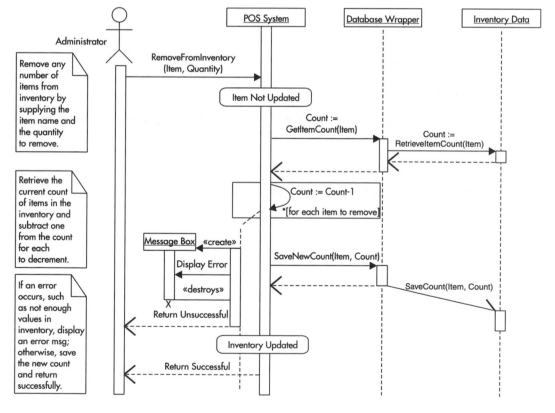

9

Further Explanation of Sequence Diagramming

Project 9-2

Further Sequence Diagram Modeling

(continued)

This is the conclusion of our discussion of sequence diagramming in this book. The topics covered in this book represent close to all the sequence diagramming techniques available from UML. As one of the easiest diagrams to construct, you should use the sequence diagram as a replacement for traditional flow charts or data flow diagrams in your current system analysis and design.

✔ Module 9 Mastery Check

1. What are some messages that would be sent during a phone call from a Telephone object and a SwitchBoard object?

2. What are some messages that would be sent during a phone call from a SwitchBoard object to a Telephone object?

3. What are some recursive calls that a Telephone object may encounter during a phone call?

4. Model a phone call using time constraints.

5. How is iteration modeled?

6. Model a phone call using iteration.

7. When an object's lifeline is not visible because it is obstructed by its control rectangle, what is inferred?

8. What is a good comment for the phone call diagram that you have created?

9. How are changes in time modeled for messages?

10. How is time duration modeled?

Module 10

Modeling Behavior with Statechart Diagrams

Statechart diagrams are very similar to activity diagrams in their notation and are sometimes confused. However, whereas an activity diagram is used to model how different areas of work behave with each other and interact, a statechart diagram is used to represent a single object and how its behavior causes it to change state.

CRITICAL SKILL
10.1 Define Statechart Diagrams

Statechart diagrams are used to model how an object changes state. *State* is defined as a snapshot or a milestone of an object's behavior at a particular point in time. For instance, the states of a computer can be defined as on, booting, processing, idle, shutting down, and off. How a computer gets from the off state to the booting state or from the processing state to the idle state is the job of statechart diagrams.

CRITICAL SKILL
10.2 Discover Why We Model Statechart Diagrams

Statechart diagrams are usually modeled for objects and some classes, to depict how an individual object changes state when its behavior is invoked. However, statechart diagrams can also be used for a number of additional reasons. For instance, a statechart diagram can be used to show how screens change state based upon user input. Statechart diagrams can also be used to show how a complex use case progresses through its states.

Progress Check

1. What is the difference between an activity diagram and a statechart diagram?

2. What is a state?

3. Why do we model statechart diagrams?

---

1. An activity diagram is used to model how different areas of work behave with each other and interact, whereas a statechart diagram is used to represent a single object and how its behavior causes it to change state.

2. State is defined as a snapshot or a milestone of a object's behavior at a particular point in time.

3. Primarily to model the changes in a object's state but they can also be used to model complex use case behavior.

CRITICAL SKILL
10.3 Identify the Notational Components
of Statechart Diagrams

A statechart diagram is composed of states, transitions, and events. States and transitions are covered in this section, and events are covered in the next section, "Learn How to Specify Actions and Events for States." By combining states and transitions, we can better model them, sometimes by including decision points and synchronization bars to show a higher level of detail.

States

There are three separate notations for states in the statechart diagram.

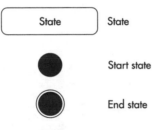

The basic state is shown as a rectangle with rounded corners. The name of the state is placed within this rectangle. This notation represents a point in the model that satisfies a condition. Examples for a diagnostic machine could be on, off, diagnosing, and idle. Names of standard states indicate what condition is met, as in the following examples.

The remaining two state notations are special cases that indicate the first and last states of the model. The first state in a model, or the start state, is simply a solid dot. The last state in a model (the end state) is a solid dot with a circle around it. A model does not need to have either a start or end state because a model can always be running and never end. Take for instance the previous examples of a diagnostic machine. What other states or activity can you picture this machine partaking in that would not be covered in this model?

A statechart diagram can include zero or more start states. A statechart diagram can include more than one end state, each showing a distinct point in which the model can terminate.

Transitions

Transitions are used to show flow from one state to another. A transition is modeled by an open arrow from one state to another. In the following notation, there is one path from the start state to the end state, which includes a stop at State A and a stop at State B.

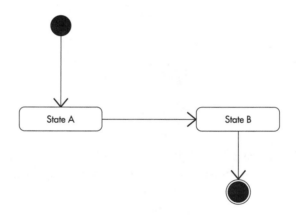

The following example of transitions illustrates a typical automatic transmission and its valid states.

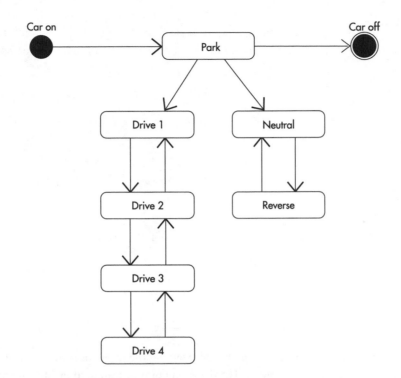

Note that this example does have a start and end state relative to the automobile being either on or off. It is possible to start the car (putting it in the Park state) and stop the car without entering any other possible state. It is not possible, however, to enter the Drive 4 state without entering the Drive 3 state.

Decision Points

Decision points are a convenience when modeling statechart diagrams, because they make the diagram more visually appealing by grouping transitions in a focal point away from the state from which they will go in their own direction. As shown in the following notation, State A can go to any of the remaining states, State B, State C, or State D. The notation for a decision point is a hollow diamond with one or more entry paths and two or more exit paths.

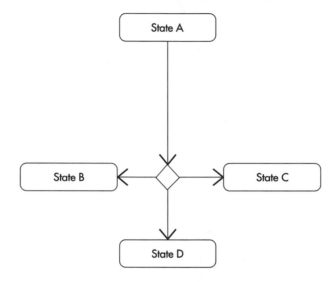

The previous illustration can be modeled by having the three transitions to each of these destination states originate at State A. The decision point is used to alleviate clutter in your diagram and can be used in cases where many transitions may be leaving a single state, not just three.

The following provides an example of using the decision state to show how navigation within a menu system can utilize the decision point. Here, the Main Menu can be used to navigate to any of the three other menus, and each of these menus can be used to navigate back to the Main Menu.

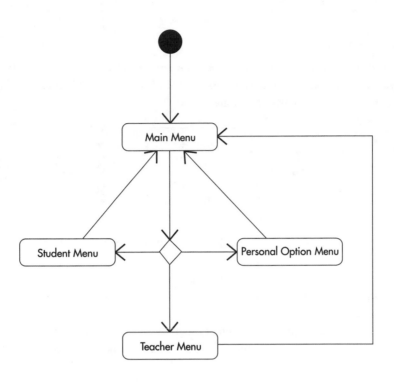

Progress Check

1. What are the two main notational components of a statechart diagram?

2. What are decision points used for?

3. What is the maximum number of start states that can be used in a statechart diagram?

---

1. States and transitions
2. To move multiple transitions from a state away from that state visually in a cluttered statechart diagram
3. There is no limit.

Synchronization

Synchronization bars are used in a statechart diagram to show where states need to catch up with or wait up for others. Synchronization bars are used to show concurrent states. The following shows the notation for synchronization bars.

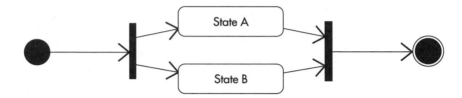

A thick bar with one transition entering it indicates the beginning of a synchronization period. Two or more transitions can exit the first synchronization bar on the other side. All synchronization bars must be paired, so they must have a way to combine back to one transition. This is shown in the reverse format where two or more transitions enter a black bar and only one transition exits.

In the following example, the statechart diagram shows that a grade has been updated, but it also shows that the grade is a failure. This state may exist because alerts or other activities may occur under this condition.

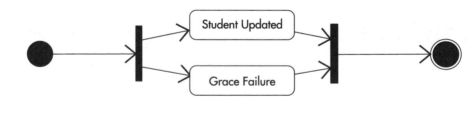

CRITICAL SKILL
10.4 Learn How to Specify Actions
and Events for States

Actions and events are used to describe how states are reached, what happens when they are reached, and what happens when they are exited. Events are used to indicate what triggers a transition, and actions are used to show what happens when an event takes place.

Events

Events are usually indicated directly on the path of a transition from a state to another state. They are used to indicate what caused the state to change in a model. The following example illustrates this notation.

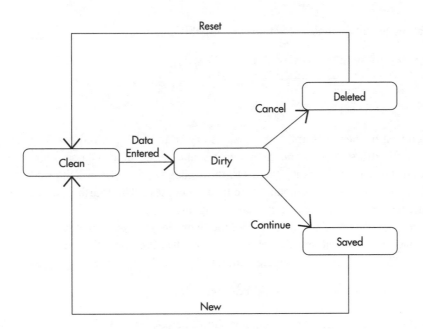

In this example, the object has four states: Clean, Dirty, Deleted, and Saved. If the object was Clean, only Data Entered can change the state and it goes directly to Dirty. From here, either the Cancel or the Continue event can change the state again to either the Deleted or the Saved state, respectively. Events can eventually be mapped to operations of a class but they do not necessarily have to have a one-to-one relationship with operations.

Actions

An action shows what behavior happens when an event occurs. There are five basic action types that a state can initiate:

- **Entry**   Used to specify the action that occurs when the state has been entered
- **Exit**   Used to specify the action that occurs when the state is being abandoned for another
- **Do**   Used to specify the activity that occurs while the state is being occupied
- **Include**   Invokes a submachine, represented by another statechart diagram
- **Event**   Used to specify the action that occurs when a specific event is fired

There are two notations for actions. The first is for the Entry, Exit, Do, and Include action types:

```
action-label / action
```

The following are examples of actions that use this notation:

```
entry / numberOfStudents = 0
exit / Classes->include(this)
do / refreshStudentList
include / performSomeSubtask
```

The first of these examples, using the entry action label, initializes the variable, numberOfStudents, to zero. The second, exit, makes sure that the Classes object includes the current instance of the current object. The third example, do, refreshes the student list by calling an operation that is meant to be local in context. The fourth and final example, include, redirects you to another statechart diagram.

The second notation for actions is for the Event action type, which is the case where you would have an event that fires the action. The event that fires the action will be from your model and most likely will only be relevant within it. The following is the notation for this action:

```
event-name (parameters) [guard-condition] / action
```

An example of the Event type of action is shown here:

```
ResetUsers(users) [Users->forAll(Open = False)] / users->empty
```

This example shows that as long as all of the users passed with the ResetUsers event are not open, they will all be removed. Do not worry too much about the expressions that are shown, because we will be exploring them in more detail in Module 12.

Of course, actions can be used in models, as we see in a slightly elaborated version of our last example.

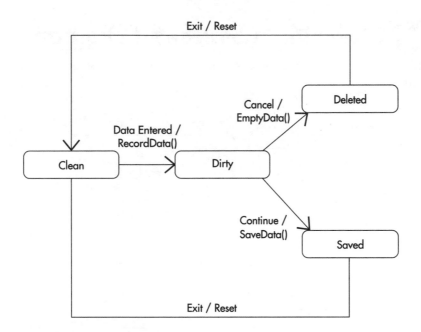

Now we see that when moving from the Clean to the Dirty state, the Data Entered event fires the RecordData action, which will most likely map to an operation within the modeled class. Once in the Dirty state, if the Cancel event is fired, the EmptyData action is also. On the other hand, if the Continue event is fired, the SaveData action is called. On exiting both the Deleted and the Saved states, the Reset action is called and the state is restored to the Clean state.

Progress Check

1. What is synchronization of states?

2. What is an event?

3. What is an action?

---

1. Allowing more than one state to be valid at a time
2. A description placed on a transition to indicate why a state is changing in a class
3. Behavior that is triggered by a condition in the state or by an event

Project 10-1 Reading a Statechart Diagram

The following statechart diagram describes the Compiler object in some detail as a project is loaded.

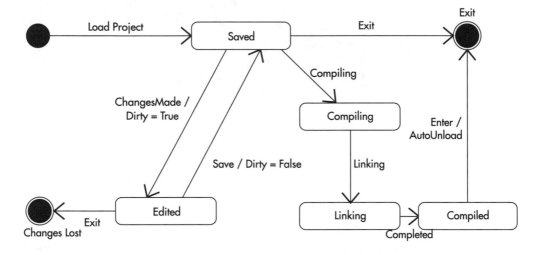

Step by Step

In the statechart diagram:

1. Identify the states.

2. Identify the transitions.

3. Identify the events and the actions.

Project Summary

This project offered a means for you to strengthen your understanding of the basic statechart notation by identifying the major components within a statechart diagram. If interpreted correctly, you would have identified not only the start and end states, but also the Saved, Edited, and Compiled states, as well as all of the transitions, events, and actions.

In the next half of this module, you will see composite states and learn how to model statechart diagrams.

CRITICAL SKILL
10.5 Understand How to Use Composite States

You have already seen that an object can have more than one state valid at a time through synchronization. Sometimes, objects can also have hierarchical states. Hierarchical states are present in a diagram when a single state can have additional substates that are unique to itself.

Substates

Substates, or states that are unique to a particular state of a diagram, can be modeled using multiple statechart diagrams, as shown in the following notation.

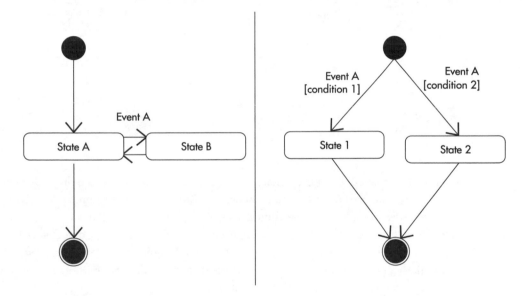

In this notation, the object can be in any one of the following sets of states:

- State A
- State B and State 1
- State B and State 2

In the left diagram of the preceding notation, Event A is causing the state of the object to change from State A to State B. In the right diagram, Event A is causing the object to also move from the start state to either State 1 or State 2 depending upon Condition 1 or Condition 2. The following example uses this exact notation to illustrate the point.

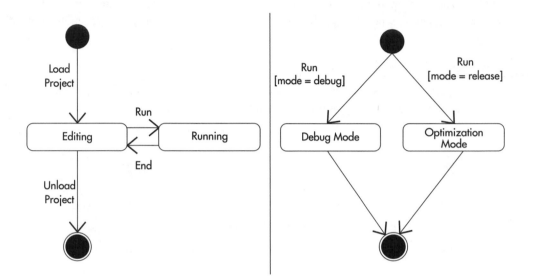

When a project is loaded, the object enters the Editing state. From there, the project can be unloaded to exit the statechart diagram, but it can also be Run to enter the Running state. The Running state is further described in the second statechart diagram, and the Run event is guarded by OCL statements that determine which transition is chosen. If the mode of the object is Debug, then the Debug state is chosen, thus making the object in the Running and Debug states at the same time. Similarly, if the mode were equal to Release, then the Optimization Mode state would also be active along with the Running state for the object.

Composite States

Another way to illustrate substates is by using the notation for composite states. Composite states are modeled by creating a very large state and embedding the substate statechart within it. This is shown in the following notation.

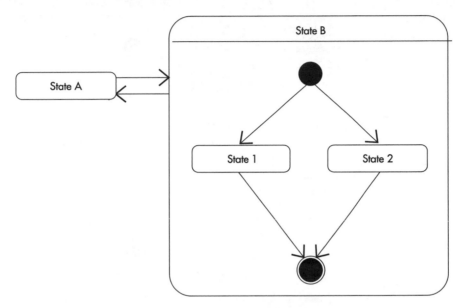

This notation shows that the following states are valid for the class being modeled:

- State A
- State B and State 1
- State B and State 2

The next example shows how composite states can be used to model substates and hierarchical states.

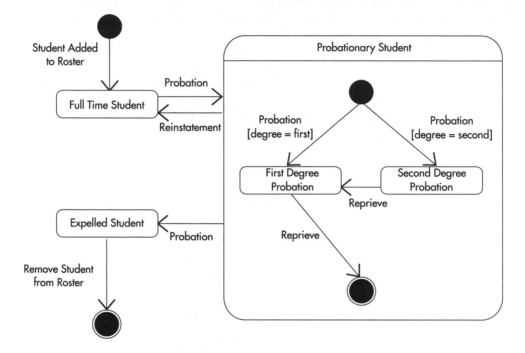

The following are the valid states (not including the start or end states) for the preceding location:

● Full Time Student

● Probationary Student and First Degree Probation

● Probationary Student and Second Degree Probation

● Expelled Student

This diagram shows that once a student is added to the roster, the Full Time Student state is valid. From here, the only way is down. A Probation event will make you a Probationary Student depending upon the severity. From there, you can get a Reprieve event and go back to being a Full Time Student, but another Probation event will get you to the Expelled Student state. Notice that a Full Time Student cannot get to Expelled Student without becoming a Probationary Student, and a Probationary Student will become an Expelled Student with a Probation event regardless of what the substate value is (First or Second Degree Probation).

Progress Check

1. What is a substate?

2. What is the difference between synchronized states and composite states?

3. How are composite states modeled?

CRITICAL SKILL
10.6 Learn How to Model State Charts

The followings steps are involved when modeling statechart diagrams:

1. Identify the entities (objects or use cases) that need to be further detailed.

2. Identify the start and end states for each entity.

3. Determine the events relating to each entity.

4. Create the statechart diagram beginning with the start event.

5. Create composite states where necessary.

These instructions mention multiple entities, but keep in mind that a statechart diagram represents a single entity. These instructions indicate that the steps need to be iterated for each entity that is involved.

Identify Entities That Need to Be Further Detailed

The first thing you need to do is identify which entities need to be further detailed with statechart diagrams. Statechart diagrams should be drawn for complex entities but not necessarily for entities with complex behavior. In this case, perhaps an activity diagram would be better suited to explain the entity's complex behavior with other entities.

---

1. A state that belongs only to a particular state in a diagram.

2. Synchronized states indicate that two or more states occur at the same time, whereas composite states show a hierarchical occurrence—where a state has other substates.

3. By placing the substate within a large state in the original statechart diagram.

Entities that have clear states that are sequential in manner are perfect candidates to be further modeled with statechart diagrams. In the following sections, we will model a Grade object, particularly its saving functionality. Perhaps this is not very complex, but it will do for our explanation.

Identify the Start and End States for the Entity

To identify the start states for an entity, you have to ask how the entity is instantiated. How does it come to life? The Grade object is instantiated when we have a new grade to save. To identify the end states for an entity, you ask the opposite question: When is this entity removed from the system? The answer for the Grade object is after it has completed its attempt to save the data, regardless of its success.

Therefore, we have found the following start and end states for the Grade object's statechart diagram depicting the save functionality:

- Information Entered start state
- Destroy end state

Determine the Events Relating to the Entity

Events ultimately become the functionality of an entity. To determine the events of an entity, you need to ask yourself what the entity does. Looking at the Grade object, we can determine that it saves the grades. Once we prod at this further (remember, we are considering the task of saving a grade to be a complex task), we can also determine that the Grade object accepts data, successfully saves data, and unsuccessfully saves data.

With these events, we can create a list of states that these events will bring us to for the Grade object:

- **Ready** For when the data has been loaded
- **Persisting** For when the data is being saved
- **Saved** For when the data has been saved
- **Error** For when the data has not been saved because of an error

Create the Statechart Diagram from the Start State

With the information that we have put together so far, we can create a simple statechart diagram that depicts the different states of the Grade object and the events that trigger the change in the states.

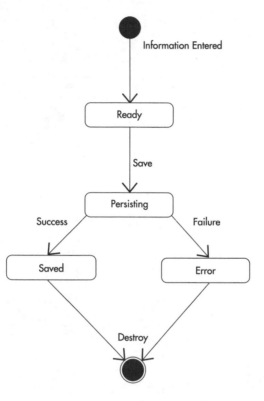

Specify Composite States Where Necessary

Once you have your first stage of your statechart diagram, you can take the time to look at it again and decide if you need to embellish on any of the states by creating composite states.

In our example, we can consider Persisting to be very general and we can go back and give it substates that would include either Load, Update and Save, or simply Insert.

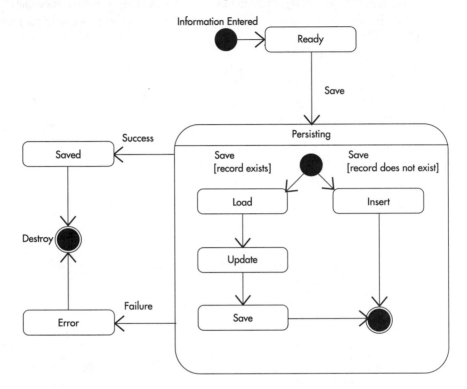

Progress Check

1. What are the steps involved in modeling a statechart diagram?

2. What question do you ask yourself to determine start and end states?

3. What question do you ask yourself to determine the events of an entity?

---

1. The steps include a) Identify the entities that need to be further detailed, b) Identify the start and end states for each entity, c) Determine the events relating to each entity, d) Create the statechart diagram beginning with the start event, and e) Create composite states where necessary.

2. How is this entity created and how is it destroyed?

3. What does this entity do?

Project 10-2 Modeling a Statechart Diagram

Project10-2_Step5.gif   Consider the point-of-sale system that we have worked with in previous modules of this book and take the single entity of Sale (a class) and create a statechart diagram describing how it accepts orders, processes them, and debits inventory upon success.

Step by Step

1. Identify the entity to model.
2. Identify the states for the entity.

NOTE

To assist you in checking your progress on this project, the diagram for this step is available online at www.osborne.com. You can easily identify this diagram available online by referencing the filename listed at the beginning of this project.

3. Identify the events that relate to the entity.
4. Model your statechart diagram.
5. Revise the statechart diagram to use substates if required.

Project Summary

You now should have successfully completed modeling your first statechart diagram. If successful, your model should look similar to this:

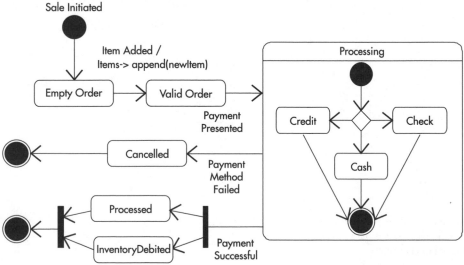

(continued)

As you probably noticed, the statechart diagram is very similar to the activity diagram, but you should not take the differences lightly. You have been able to create a diagram that has described the behavior of a single entity in terms of how it changes states internally.

Module 10 Mastery Check

1. What are the basic notational components of statechart diagrams?

2. What is the difference between statechart diagrams and activity diagrams?

3. What does synchronization accomplish in statechart diagrams?

4. What is the difference between events and actions?

5. What are the steps involved in diagramming a statechart diagram?

6. What is a substate?

7. How is a composite state modeled?

8. What are the five basic types of actions?

9. What are the two different notations for actions?

10. What are decision points used for?

Module 11

Architecting with Implementation Diagrams

233

Implementation diagrams are used to show where the physical components of a system are going to be placed in relation to each other, the hardware, or the Internet. Implementation diagrams can be written early on in the UML process to get an idea of what is needed for rolling out the finished product, but they cannot be formalized until your software has been completely modeled with Class diagrams.

CRITICAL SKILL

11.1 Define Implementation Diagrams

The two types of implementation diagrams are component diagrams and deployment diagrams. Component diagrams are modeled to illustrate relationships between pieces of software, while deployment diagrams are modeled to illustrate relationships between pieces of hardware.

CRITICAL SKILL

11.2 Discover Why We Model Implementation Diagrams

We model implementation diagrams to give the reader, whether that be the product manager, the developer, or even someone from quality assurance, an understanding of where the pieces of a system are located and how they interact. Our system is a piece of software when we are using UML to design.

The component diagram is used to model the relationships between pieces of a system (including source code, binaries, executables, scripts, or command files) that are grouped by functionality or location (file). We use component diagrams to help understand where functionality is located in a software package and which version of a software package contains which pieces of functionality.

A deployment diagram, on the other hand, illustrates to the reader where each piece of the software will reside on hardware, and how those pieces of hardware interact with each other. Deployment diagrams can also be used to record which software is installed on which hardware.

Implementation diagrams in general can be used to help design the overall architecture of a system.

CRITICAL SKILL

11.3 Learn about Component Diagrams

Component diagrams model software components and their relationships with each other. These diagrams are made up of component notations and relationships between each component.

Components

To model a component, we use a rectangle with two small rectangles on the left edge.

A component is a single piece of software. It can be a file, product, executable, script, or so on. In the following example, we illustrate some files that can be modeled with the component notation. We use the Visual Basic file extensions to illustrate a project file, a module file, and a class file.

Dependencies

Dependencies are used to illustrate relationships between two components. We model dependencies with a dashed line with an open arrow at one end. The arrow is drawn from the object that is dependent to the object that it depends on. The following example would be read as ComponentA depends upon ComponentB.

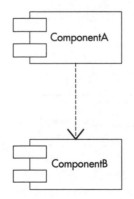

Revisiting our previous example of a Visual Basic project and two source files, we can relate each source file to the project file by using the dependency notation.

The following example diagrams that the Project file depends upon both the Global.bas and Collection.cls files.

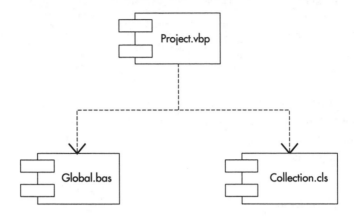

Stereotyping Dependencies

A dependency can be stereotyped to give meaning to the relationship. The notation for stereotyping a component dependency is to write the name of the stereotype in guillemets («...»).

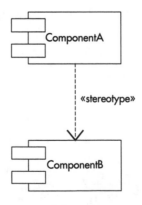

A popular stereotype is «includes», as shown in the following example where we indicate that the Project.vbp file includes both the Global.bas file and the Collection.cls file.

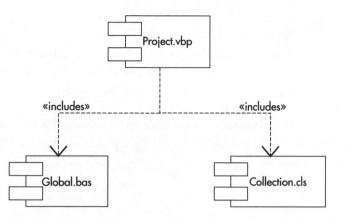

Although «includes» is commonly used, you can use any stereotyped name that you feel best describes the relationship for your system that you are modeling. Some other examples of stereotype names include «imports» and «implements».

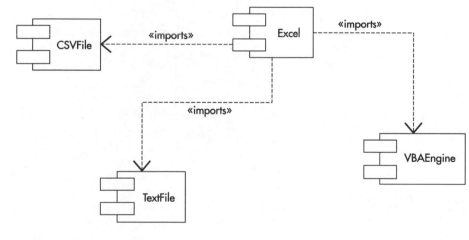

TIP

A good way to come up with stereotype names is to put the component relationship in a sentence. In the preceding example, we read the dependency between the Excel and the VBAEngine components as "Excel implements VBAEngine." We start off saying "Excel does what with the VBAEngine?" Other valid stereotype names for this component relationship would include «has», «contains», and «supports».

Contained Components

Components can be contained within other components. This notation is diagrammed by actually modeling components inside other components. There is no limit to the number of levels you can nest components, but keep in mind that the purpose of UML is to make things clear, so be careful to not confuse the reader.

The following model illustrates that the Inventory component is composed of three individual components, DataAccess, Business Logic, and UserInterface—the three tiers of an enterprise system.

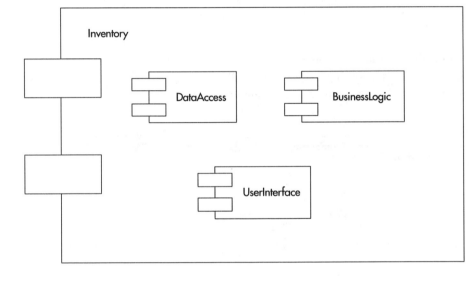

Progress Check

1. What is a component diagram?

2. What is a deployment diagram?

3. What are the relationships between components called?

---

1. A model of software components in a system
2. A model of how hardware is deployed in a system
3. Dependencies

Project 11-1 Reading a Component Diagram

In this project, you will interpret the following component diagram by recognizing the UML notation you have learned so far in this module. You will identify the individual components, the container components and their contained components, the dependencies between the components, and the stereotypes used to describe these dependencies.

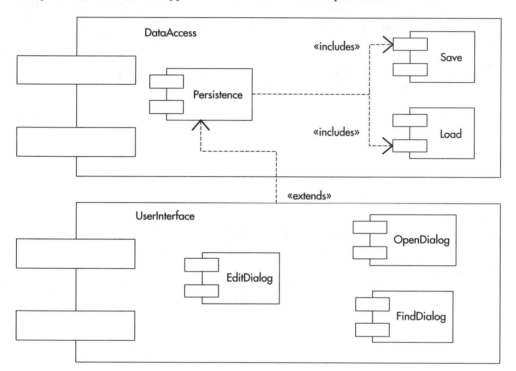

Step by Step

For this project's component diagram:

1. Identify the components.

2. Identify the contained components.

3. Identify the dependencies.

4. Identify the stereotypes.

(continued)

Project Summary

In this project, you should have successfully identified the notations used to model component diagrams. You should have been able to recognize components and their relationships to each other by simply reading a model. You should have identified the components Save, Load, and Persistence, among others, as well as the dependencies that a Persistence component depends on the Save and Load components.

In the next section, we will take a look at deployment diagrams.

CRITICAL SKILL
11.4 Learn about Deployment Diagrams

While component diagrams are used to model software components, deployment diagrams are used to model hardware as it relates to the deployment of the system that you are modeling in UML. A deployment diagram has only two major pieces of its notation, the node and the communication association.

Nodes

A node is used to represent a piece of hardware, whether it be a printer, computer, scanner, or telephone pole. The notation for a node is a three-dimensional box that contains the name of the node in the upper-left corner.

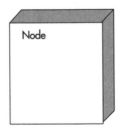

Nodes can be modeled as a generic form of a piece of hardware, such as a WebServer, Scanner, or Router. They can also be modeled as a specific instance of a piece of hardware, by changing the notation of the node name much like you would change the notation of a class to an object.

In the following illustration, the top three nodes are generic, while the bottom three nodes are instances of the generic nodes. The instantiated nodes have their name underlined and are trailed by a colon and the name of the generic node that is implemented.

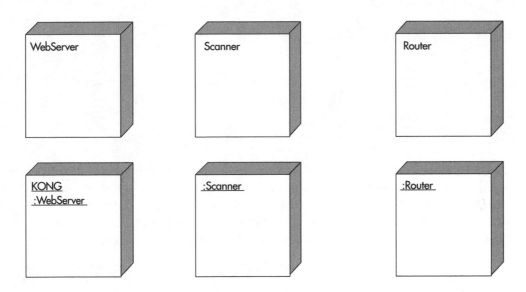

In the previous example, KONG is the name of a WebServer. There is only one KONG, but there are many WebServers. Both the Scanner and the Router node instances do not have particular names because they are of no importance to the model that they are included in. By the underlined text and the colon, the reader can understand that this is an instantiated node without a name specified.

TIP

To know when to model a node instance, ask yourself whether the model is going to diagram information specific to an individual occurrence of a node or information that is general to all instances of a node.

Communication Associations

Nodes are related with communication associations, solid lines that are drawn from one node to another. This relationship is used to identify that the two pieces of hardware (nodes) communicate with each other by some means, which is indicated in the stereotype that is always shown with a communication association.

Architecting with Implementation Diagrams

11

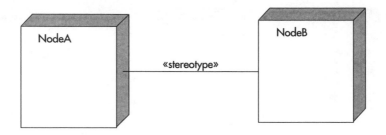

Stereotypes for communication associations are notated just like stereotypes for component dependencies, with guillemets («...»). The stereotype name usually is something that describes the method of communication, or protocol, between the two pieces of hardware.

The following diagram illustrates that a WebServer interacts with a ClientPC via an HTTP protocol, and the ClientPC communicates with a Printer via a USB protocol.

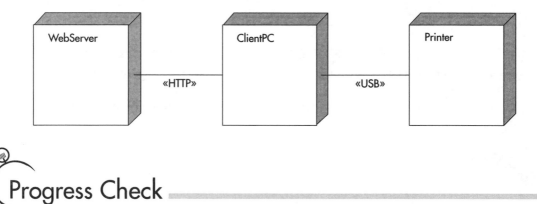

Progress Check

1. How do you model an instance of a node?

2. What does a communication association model?

3. What do communication association stereotypes model?

---

1. With a three-dimensional box that includes the name of the instance, a colon, and the name of the general node that has been instantiated

2. Communication between two pieces of hardware

3. The protocol used to communicate between the two pieces of hardware

Project 11-2 Reading a Deployment Diagram

In this project, you will interpret the following deployment diagram by recognizing the UML notation that you have learned so far in this module. You will identify the generic nodes, the instantiated nodes, and the association communications between the nodes.

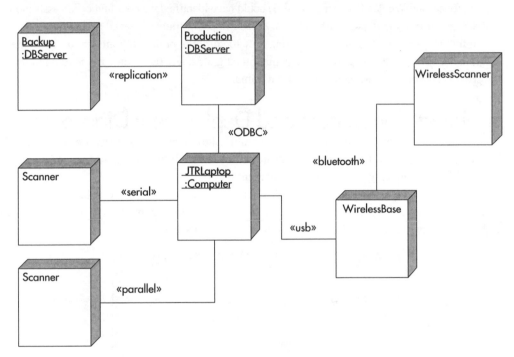

Step by Step

For this project's deployment diagram:

1. Identify the generic nodes.

2. Identify the instantiated nodes.

3. Identify the communication associations.

(continued)

Project Summary

This project should have helped you identify the difference between generic nodes, instantiated nodes, and the communication associations that are used to indicate the relationships between the two different node types. You should have been able to identify the generic nodes Scanner, WirelessBase, and WirelessScanner. You also should have identified the communication associations that a Scanner communicates with both the JTRLaptop:Computer in serial and parallel.

In the next section, you will be learning how to combine both component and deployment diagrams to give you the ultimate implementation diagrams, and then you will move on to learn how to model your own implementation diagrams.

Combining Component and Deployment Diagrams

Component and deployment diagrams can be combined to illustrate how software is distributed, or will be distributed, over a particular hardware configuration. When both hardware and software are combined, technically you have a deployment diagram.

Components can be modeled as parts of a node (software can be modeled as being installed on or in a piece of hardware). The following diagram shows how the Communications, BusinessLogic, and Scan components are all located in the Scanner hardware.

Another way to model that software is located on a piece of hardware is to include dependencies from the hardware (node) to the software (component). These dependencies (drawn with dashed lines and open arrows) can be stereotyped just as when they are used to relate two components.

The following diagram shows that the ClientComputer includes the UserInterface and BusinessLogic components, while the ServerComputer (which communicates with the ClientComputer over a WAN) includes the DatabaseRoutines and the BackendFunctionality.

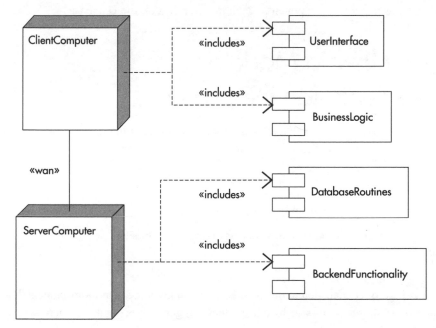

This diagram can also be drawn using the nodes as containers for the components.

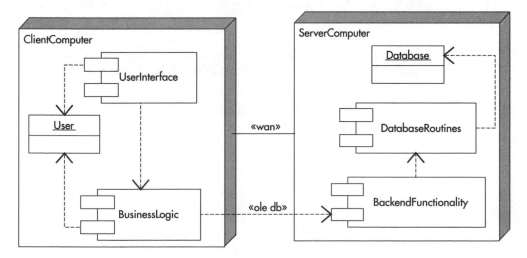

In this diagram, we have added a couple of class instances (objects) to show where they reside. This model shows that the UserInterface and the BusinessLogic components depend on the User object, all of which reside on the ClientComputer. Connected to the ServerComputer via a WAN, the ClientComputer's BusinessLogic component communicates with the ServerComputer's BackendFunctionality component with OLE DB. The BackendFunctionality component depends on the DatabaseRoutines component, which in turn relies on the Database.

CRITICAL SKILL
11.5 Learn How to Model Implementation Diagrams

The Unified Process indicates that there are four tasks for creating implementation diagrams after you know what you plan on modeling:

1. Add nodes.

2. Add communication associations.

3. Add components and other things such as classes and objects.

4. Add dependencies.

We will go over each step in this process in detail using a set of requirements that we will assume has been prepared for us by our product manger, subject matter expert, and whoever else wanted to be involved.

Our overall requirement is to model an implementation diagram for the architecture of a system used to scan products to be retrieved by clients via the Web. Our more detailed requirements are as follows:

- A scanner is used to scan product information. The scanner is connected to a network card via an internal PCI bus. Code will be written to control the scanner and it will reside within the unit itself.

- The network card from the scanner will communicate, via radio waves, to a wireless hub that will be plugged into our web server, KONG, which will serve pages via HTTP to client PCs.

- The web server machine will house our custom web server software that interacts with our product database via a proprietary data access component.

- On the client's PC, we will provide a proprietary browser that only interacts with our custom web server, running a product lookup add-in control.

Add Nodes

The first task is to identify the nodes of our system. To do this, we have to scan our requirements to come up with a list of all the hardware that we can find. The following illustration shows the generic hardware pieces identified in the previous requirements.

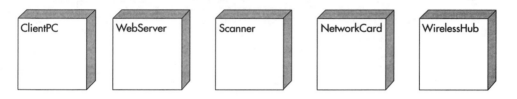

Add Communication Associations

Next, we have to relate the nodes that we have identified with communication associations. Since communication associations are stereotyped to indicate the type of communication between the nodes, we also need to search the requirements for this information. We can identify, from our requirements, the following communication associations:

- A scanner is connected to a network card via an internal PCI bus.

- A network card communicates with a wireless hub via radio waves.

- A wireless hub is connected to an instance of a web server called KONG via USB.

- The KONG web server communicates with client computers via HTTP.

While identifying the communication associations, we have decided that our WebServer node can be instantiated, because we are dealing with a single instance of the server called KONG. The following diagram puts our identified communication associations in place.

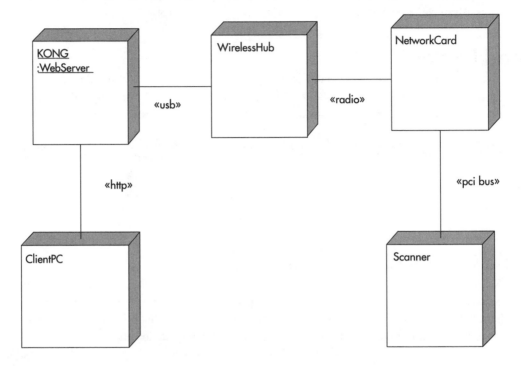

Add Components, Classes, and Objects

Next, we want to identify our components and other pieces such as classes and objects. The requirements listed the following components that we can use in our diagram:

- Code written to control the scanner (named ScanEngine component)
- Custom web server (named WebServerSoft component)
- Proprietary data access component (named DataAccess component)
- Proprietary browser (named Browser component)
- Product lookup add-in control (named ProductLookupAddIn component)

In addition, a product database was mentioned, but this may not necessarily be a software component that we want to model in the same way as the preceding items. Instead, we can model the product database as a class instance (an object). We will call this ProductDB for short.

We can add the components and the object to the diagram we created in the previous step by placing the ScanEngine component inside the Scanner node; by placing the Browser and

ProductLookupAddIn components within the ClientPC node; and by placing the DataAccess component, WebServerSoft component, and ProductDB object within the KONG node instance.

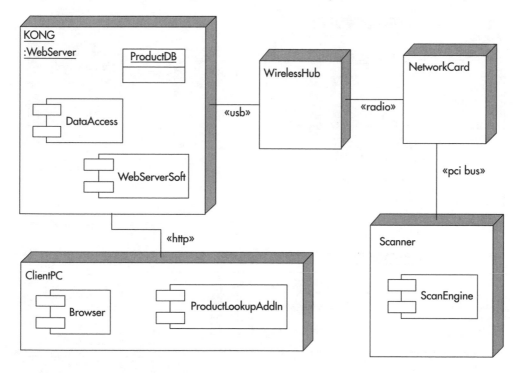

Add Dependencies

To add the finishing touches to our implementation diagram, we will model the dependencies between the components and object that we have added. Once again, we look to the requirements to identify this information.

The custom web server software (WebServerSoft component) interacts with our product database (ProductDB) via a proprietary component indicating the following dependencies:

● The WebServerSoft component depends upon the DataAccess component.

● The DataAccess component depends upon the ProductDB object.

The proprietary browser only interacts with our custom web server running a product lookup add-in control. This indicates to us the following dependencies:

● The Browser component depends upon the WebServerSoft component.

● The ProductLookupAddIn component depends upon the Browser component.

Together, this gives us four dependencies that we can model as shown in the following illustration.

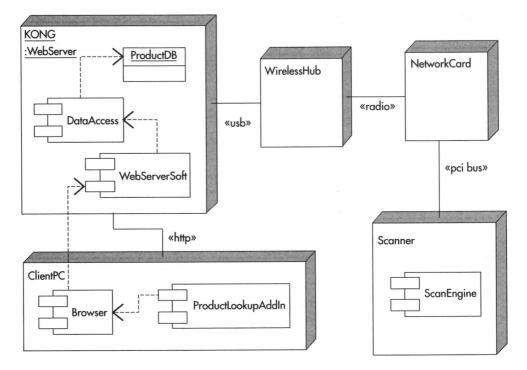

Now you have stepped through the stages of modeling your first implementation diagram based upon requirements. It wasn't that hard after all. In the next section, you will be given the chance to model your own implementation diagram on your own.

Progress Check

1. How do you identify nodes from requirements?

2. How do you model that software is installed on a piece of hardware?

3. What are some other things that you can model in an implementation diagram besides components and nodes?

---

1. Find all the pieces of hardware mentioned
2. By modeling a component within a node
3. Objects and classes

Project 11-3 Model an Implementation Diagram

```
Project11-3_Step1.gif
Project11-3_Step2.gif
Project11-3_Step3.gif
```

In this project, you will take the business requirements listed next and create an implementation diagram for them. You will leverage your knowledge of the UML notation for component and deployment diagrams, including components, dependencies, nodes, and communication associations. You will also use information that you have learned in previous modules on classes and objects.

The following requirements are for a Kiosk system:

- An instance of a Kiosk will communicate over a T1 line to the KONG central receiver server. The Kiosk will send information from its send request software to KONG's receive request software.

- The Kiosk will maintain an instance of a SearchByPortal class and a SearchByManufacture class, which will be used by the send request software to process requests on the KONG server.

- The KONG server in turn will process the requests by the receive request functionality that includes a data access component.

- The data access component will access both a product server and a manufacturer server. KONG will have access to both of these servers via a wide area network.

- An instance of a product database resides on the product server, and an instance of the manufacturer database resides on the manufacturer server. Both databases are pushed information by update products code running on an additional application server.

- The application server connects to the product server, the product server connects to the manufacturer server, and the manufacturer server connects to KONG, all via the WAN.

- The application server also contains a validation component that is used by the update products code.

Step by Step

1. Identify the nodes of the system.

NOTE

To assist you in checking your progress on this project, diagrams for selected steps are available online at www.osborne.com. You can easily identify the diagrams available online by referencing the filenames listed at the beginning of this project.

2. Identify the communication associations of the system.

(continued)

3. Identify the components, classes, and objects of the system.

4. Identify the dependencies of the system.

Project Summary

In this project, you should have successfully created an implementation diagram from only the requirements supplied to you. If successful, your diagram should look similar to the following:

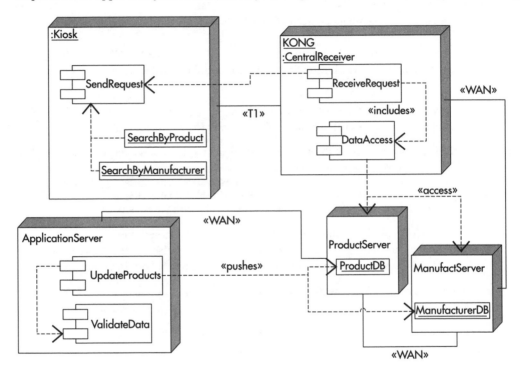

Again, you should congratulate yourself as you continue on your path toward excellence in UML knowledge! In the next module, the last in this book, we will take a look at the Object Constraint Language (OCL).

Module 11 Mastery Check

1. What is the difference between a component and a deployment diagram?

2. What do components represent?

3. What are the relationships between components called?

4. What is the purpose of modeling contained components?

5. What do nodes represent?

6. What are the relationships between nodes called?

7. List the steps to create an implementation diagram.

8. What is meant by stereotyping dependencies?

9. List some nodes that can be found in your home network.

10. List some components of a client-server application.

Module 12

Using the Object
Constraint Language

The Object Constraint Language is a means of indicating limitations within your modeled system. It is an optional addition to UML that can be used to better define the behavior of your objects. With OCL, one can define attributes such as minimum, maximum, default, and acceptable ranges for data that the system will use.

CRITICAL SKILL
2.1 Define Object Constraint Language (OCL)

So what exactly is the Object Constraint Language? To answer this question, let us first break down the name. The word "object" represents a component of your system. It is the item that is being better defined. The word "constraint" represents a limitation, such as the maximum number of people allowed to log on to a web page (object) at a time, or perhaps the highest grade (object) that a student can get. The "language" portion of the name does not represent a formal computer language, but instead refers to a less formal language that can be applied to any implementation.

OCL has no control over any other component of a UML diagram; it simply returns a value when used. The responsibility lies with the developer to code the proper functionality based upon the return value of an OCL statement. In other words, OCL can't be used to change the state of an object, but it can be used to indicate when a change in state will occur. Changing the state occurs during development by utilizing the return value of an OCL statement.

CRITICAL SKILL
2.2 Discover Why We Use OCL

OCL can be used to define the pre- and post-conditions for functionality modeled in your system. It can be used to describe guards used throughout your diagrams or transitions from one object to another in other diagrams. OCL can also be used to describe *invariants* of a system, properties that must remain true throughout the lifetime of a system. For instance, a student's grade point average must not be higher than 4.0.

The language itself has been defined for the same reason UML has been defined—to give one clear method for presenting your model, in this case, the constraints of your model.

Progress Check

1. What does OCL stand for?

2. What is a constraint?

3. What can OCL be used for?

---

1. Object Constraint Language
2. A limitation
3. To define pre- and post-conditions of a use case, to describe guards and transitions, and to describe invariants of a system

CRITICAL SKILL
12.3 Understand OCL Syntax

OCL specifies that every constraint must have a context. A *context* indicates what item is being constrained. The constraint itself acts like an expression so that it evaluates to a specific type (such as a number or a True or False value). OCL is a typed language, meaning that data types play an important role. Just as with a high-level language such as C++ or Visual Basic, you cannot divide a String value by a Boolean with OCL.

Context and Stereotypes

The context of a constraint written in OCL can be a class or an operation. Once you understand the context of a constraint, you need to specify the stereotype of the constraint. The stereotype of the constraint can be one of three choices:

- «pre-condition»

- «post-condition»

- «invariant»

Pre- and post-condition constraints are used for operations, while invariant constraints are used for classes. Notice how stereotypes are enclosed in guillemets (« »).

A pre-condition is a value that needs to be True before the context of a constraint can be realized, while a post-condition is a value that needs to be True before the context of a constraint can be considered completed. An invariant, as we said earlier, is a value that must remain True for the life of the context.

To represent a simple OCL constraint statement, the notation is as follows:

```
context context inv:
    constraint
```

Notice that the words *context* and *constraint* are in italics. The two values that must be inserted into this notation are the actual context and the actual constraint or list of constraints. The following example illustrates this:

```
context Student inv:
    GPA <= 4.0
```

This OCL statement demands that the Student classes' GPA attribute always be less than or equal to 4.0.

If the class that is being depicted as the context of a constraint is part of a package, that can also be specified, as in the following example:

```
context Teachers::SocialStudiesTeacher inv:
    AssignedClasses->includes(GlobalStudies)
```

This last constraint ensures that every Social Studies Teacher (part of the Teachers package) has a Global Studies class belonging to their Assigned Classes attribute. Don't worry about the particulars regarding the use of the exists operation in this last example; we will go over this later in this module, in the "Discover the Use of Collections" section.

Progress Check

1. What are the three stereotypes used on a constraint's context?

2. Which stereotype(s) can be used for classes?

3. Which stereotype(s) can be used for operations?

To represent a constraint for an operation, you would replace the context value with the name and complete parameter list of the operation. This is necessary because operations can be overloaded and only become unique when their parameter list is included.

```
context operation(parameters) : return
    pre: constraint
    post: constraint
```

The preceding notation shows how the pre- and post-conditions are indicated on separate lines and are preceded by the text pre: and post:, both in bold type. The following example illustrates the use of both pre- and post-conditions within a constraint statement:

```
context SocialStudiesTeacher::AddHighSchoolClass(Class, Grade) : Success
    pre: Grade >= 9
    pre: Grade <= 12
    post: classes.includes(Class)
```

1. «pre-condition», «post-condition», and «invariant»
2. «invariant»
3. «pre-condition» and «post-condition»

This example adds a couple of things. We indicate which class the AddHighSchoolClass belongs to (SocialStudiesTeacher) and we use two pre-condition constraints. The grade that is being passed into the AddHighSchoolClass needs to be between 9 and 12 as a pre-condition for the operation to be able to perform its functionality. A developer should be able to read this statement and include error-checking functionality to immediately detect whether the grade is the correct level, and if it isn't, the operation shouldn't continue. Assuming the grade is correct, and the operation does execute, the result of the functionality would be that the specified Class would be now included in the classes collection for that teacher.

Types and Operations

As we discussed earlier in this module, OCL is a typed language. This means that data types of attributes, parameters, and return values are very important to how OCL is constructed. There are four basic types belonging to OCL:

● Integer

● Real

● String

● Boolean

Integer numbers are any whole numbers (without a fraction) such as 3, 2, 1, 0, –1 and –2. Real numbers are any number that you can imagine (with or without a fraction) such as 3.0, 2.34, 1.1, 0.0, –1.5, and –2.45. Integers can be Real numbers but Real numbers cannot be Integers. String values include any amount of text data such as "Jason Rocks" or "a". A Boolean value can either be True or False.

There are many operations that can be used with these four types:

● =, < >, <, >, <=, >=, +, –, *, /, max( ), or min( ) can be used on two Integer or Real values

● mod( ) and div( ) can only be used on two Integer values

● abs, round, and floor can only be used on one Integer or Real value

● or, and, xor, < >, or implies can be used on two Boolean values

● concat( ), =, or < > can be used on two String values

● size, toLower, or toUpper can be used on one String value

The following list shows some examples of the least common operators:

● (4).max(3) = 4

● (5).min(3) = 3

- (3).mod(2) = 1
- (3).div(2) = 1
- (3.53).abs = 3
- (3.53).round = 4
- (3.53).floor = 3
- True or False = True
- True and False = False
- True xor False = True
- 'Jason'.concat('rocks') = 'Jason rocks'
- 'Zachary'.size = 7
- 'Zachary rocks'.toUpper = 'ZACHARY ROCKS'

Progress Check

1. What are the four types native to OCL?

2. What types can be used with mod( ) and div( ) operations?

3. Why must a parameter list be included in the context of an operation?

You can, of course, use attributes in place of any of the four types that you just learned about within a constraint, as shown in the earlier examples. For instance, if a teacher must have at least five classes, we can show this as the following constraint:

```
context Teacher inv:
    totalClassCount >= 5
```

A type does not always have to be the standard four that are defined in OCL. Nor do the operations that you use on other types need to be defined in OCL. Your model defines additional types, which can include attributes and classes. Classes, in turn, can define additional operations that can be used in your OCL modeling.

---

1. Integer, Real, String, and Boolean
2. Integer only
3. Because operations can be overloaded and it is necessary to uniquely define the operation

Take, for instance, the following example that shows that the SocialStudiesTeacher class has an invariant condition that implies that the total working hours (based upon the teacher's classes) must be less than or equal to 8. totalWorkingHours must be a function of the SocialStudiesTeacher class that returns an Integer or a Real number.

```
context SocialStudiesTeacher inv:
    self.totalWorkingHours(Classes) <= 8
```

Project 12-1 Reading Basic OCL

From the following notation, identify and list the different components in the OCL:

```
context Compiler inv:
    System::OSVersion >= 2000
    System::FreeHDSpace >= 1500
    Libraries->includes(CoreLibraries)
context Compiler::Compile(projectName, files, options) : Success
    pre: projectName.size <> 0
    pre: files.size <> 0
    pre: if (options->includes(debug)) then options->includes(debugversion)
    post: (Success = True) or
          ((Success = False) and (Errors::Description=self.Error))
```

Step by Step

1. List the invariant constraints.

2. List the pre-conditions.

3. List the post-conditions.

Project Summary

Congratulations on successfully completing your first OCL reading task. This project questioned and confirmed your understanding of the basic OCL notation and ability within a model. If successful, you would have identified the following:

● The first invariant constraint of the Compiler class requires that the System class's OSVersion attribute must be set to 2000 or higher.

● The next invariant constraint of the Compiler class requires that the System class's FreeHDSpace attribute must be set to 1500 or higher.

● The final invariant constraint of the Compiler class requires that the Libraries collection must include the CoreLibraries type.

(continued)

- The first pre-condition of the Compile operation of the Compiler class requires that the project name exists.

- The second pre-condition requires that files exist.

- The third pre-condition specifies that if the debug option exists in the options collection, then the debug version option also needs to exist.

- The post-condition for the Compile operation of the Compiler class requires that the return value must be set to True; otherwise, if it is set to False, the Error needs to be set to the Errors class's Description attribute.

Now that you understand the basics, we will move on to explain a little more about the collections that you've been seeing so far.

Discover the Use of Collections

A collection is a group of items that are somehow related, possibly sorted and ordered and possibly having business rules associated with them to enforce which type of items are allowed in the collection. Collections can be manipulated through the use of operations to report on or to change their contents. There are three types of collections in OCL:

- Sets

- Sequences

- Bags

Each varies slightly and each behaves differently when using the OCL collection operations.

Sets

A set is a distinct list of items that is unordered. A set is written with the following notation:

```
set{items in the set}
```

For instance, a set of Integers could look like this:

```
set{1, 9, 4, -1, 0}
```

A set of String values could look like this:

```
set{'zachary', 'kimberly', 'jason'}
```

Taking the last set, we can apply a collection operation called including, which simply appends the new item to the set if it doesn't already exist:

```
collection->including('roxy') = set{'zachary', 'kimberly', 'jason', 'roxy'}
```

The excluding operation removes a name from the set if it exists. Assuming we are starting with the original set, the following would remove 'jason' from the set:

```
collection->excluding('jason') = set{'zachary', 'kimberly'}
```

Sometimes, applying an operation to a collection results in a different type of collection. The union operation does just that. It adds all the occurrences of one set to the occurrences of another. Because an item can appear in both sets, the result can contain duplicates of a particular item, which is no longer a set. This is called a *bag*, an unordered list of items that allows repetition. (Bags will be explained in the upcoming section after we discuss sequences.) The following example shows how the union of two sets results in a bag:

```
(set{'jason', 'kimberly'})->union(set{'kimberly', 'zachary'}) =
    bag{'jason', 'kimberly', 'kimberly', 'zachary'}
```

Sequences

A sequence is a list of items that is ordered and that allows repetition. Sequences are displayed very similarly to sets, as shown here:

```
sequence{items in the sequence}
```

The items in the sequence give no hint to the reader that their order is important. Instead, it is up to the word sequence to indicate this:

```
sequence{4, 9, 2, 0, 1, -23, 2}
```

Because the sequence is the only collection that cares about the order of its items, it has a couple of unique operations that can be used. The first and last operations simply retrieve the first and last items in the sequence:

```
(sequence{4, 9, 2, 0, 1, -23, 2})->first = 4
(sequence{4, 9, 2, 0, 1, -23, 2})->last = 2
```

The append and prepend operations add data to the beginning of a sequence and to the end of a sequence, respectively:

```
(sequence{4, 2, 1, 3})->append(0) = sequence{0, 4, 2, 1, 3}
(sequence{4, 2, 1, 3})->prepend(0) = sequence{4, 2, 1, 3, 0}
```

Bags

As mentioned earlier, a bag is an unordered list of items that also allows repetition. A bag is displayed in a similar fashion to the other two collections:

```
bag{items in the bag}
```

A bag can use the union operation just as a set collection can:

```
(bag{1, 2, 3, 4})->union(bag(3, 3, 3, 3}) = bag{1, 2, 3, 3, 3, 3, 3, 4}
```

A bag can use the intersection operation to produce a set that contains only the items common to both bags, but without repetition:

```
(bag{1, 2, 3, 4})->intersection(bag(3, 3, 3, 3}) = set{3}
```

Another useful function of a bag is the asSet operation, which removes the duplicates from a bag:

```
(bag{1, 1, 2, 2, 3, 3,})->asSet = set{1, 2, 3}
```

Progress Check

1. What is a set?

2. What is a sequence?

3. What is a bag?

Other Common Operations Used on Collections

The operations that you have learned so far in this module are by far not the complete list of operations that can be used in OCL. Listing and explaining every operation would be outside the scope of this book. Instead, I will go over a few operations that are commonly used and that will be helpful to you in your OCL modeling.

The select operation is useful with all collections to produce a collection based upon a given criteria. It returns the same type of collection that is passed to it:

```
(set{1, 2, 3, 4, 5})->select(x | x > 3) = set{4, 5}
```

---

1. A distinct list of items that is unordered
2. A list of items that is ordered and allows repetition
3. An unordered list of items that also allows repetition

The reject operation is the opposite of the select operation in that it returns the collection that satisfies where an expression is false:

```
(set{1, 2, 3, 4, 5})->reject(x | x > 3) = set{1, 2, 3}
```

The forall operation returns a Boolean value of True if every element in the collection satisfies an expression:

```
(set{1, 2, 3, 4, 5})->forall(x | x > 3) = False
```

The exists operation evaluates to True if at least one item in the collection satisfies the expression:

```
(set{1, 2, 3, 4, 5})->exists(x | x > 3) = True
```

The size operation returns the number of items in the collection:

```
(set{1, 2, 3, 4, 5})->size = 5
```

The count operation returns the number of items in the collection that are equivalent to the item passed to the operation:

```
(set{1, 2, 3, 4, 5})->count(3) = 1
```

The isEmpty operation returns True if the collection has no items in it:

```
(set{1, 2, 3, 4, 5})->isEmpty = False
```

Progress Check

1. What does the forall operation do?

2. What does the reject operation do?

3. What does the count operation do?

1. Returns a Boolean value of True if every element in the collection satisfies an expression
2. Returns the collection that satisfies where an expression is False
3. Returns the number of items in the collection that are equivalent to the item passed to the operation

Project 12-2 Reading Advanced OCL

Prepare the OCL for the StudentGrades class' AddGrade and CalculateGPA operations. The following business rules apply to these cases:

- The student must be loaded and initialized in the class before you can use it.

- Grades should be kept in two categories, tests and assignments.

- A grade cannot be added for a test or assignment if it already exists.

- The student must have at least one grade to calculate a GPA.

- The AddGrade operation needs to call the NotifyParents function if the GPA falls below a 2.0.

Step by Step

1. Create the invariant constraints.

2. Create the pre-conditions.

3. Create the post-conditions.

Project Summary

That is it for the OCL training in this module...and that is it for this book on UML. At this time, you have achieved success in being able to interpret both basic and complex OCL constraint statements that include the basic OCL types, custom types used from your model and and custom types used with collections that have their own set of operations.

✓

Module 12 Mastery Check

1. What are the three stereotypes of a constraint and what is the context of each?

2. List the operations used for Integers.

3. List the operations used for Reals.

4. List the operations used for Booleans.

5. List the operations used for Strings.

6. What are the three types of collections in OCL and what are the differences?

7. List some operations used for all types of collections.

8. Evaluate

```
(bag{True, False, True, False})->union(bag{True})
```

9. Evaluate

```
(sequence{'zachary', 'kimberly', 'jason'})->last
```

10. Evaluate

```
(set{'jason', 'rocks'})->excluding('rolls')
```

11. Evaluate

```
(set{True, false})->including(True)
```

12. Evaluate

```
(set{'jason', 'rocks'})->excluding('rocks')
```

13. Evaluate

```
(set{1, 2})->union(set{0})
```

14. Evaluate

```
(sequence{'zachary', 'kimberly', 'jason'})->first
```

15. Evaluate

```
(sequence{1, 2, 2, 3, 0})->last
```

16. Evaluate

```
(sequence{1, 2, 3, 4})->append(sequence{5})
```

17. Evaluate

```
(bag{'jason', 'jason', 'jason'})->asSet
```

18. Evaluate

```
(bag{True, False, True, False})->intersection(bag{True})
```

Appendix A

Answers to Mastery Checks

Module 1: UML Fundamentals

1. **Why do we model software?**

   To achieve a high level of quality in the final software product.

2. **What are the three major steps to modeling software?**

   Analysis, design, and implementation

3. **What are the three major software lifecycle models?**

   Waterfall, spiral, and iterative-incremental

4. **What are the four phases of the Unified Process?**

   Inception, elaboration, construction, and transition

5. **Who are the three major contributors to UML?**

   Grady Booch, Jim Rumbaugh, and Ivar Jacobson

6. **What was the first version of UML?**

   UML 0.8

7. **What does the acronym OMG stand for and what does OMG do?**

   Object Management Group—sets vendor-neutral software standards

8. **What are the types of structural diagrams within UML?**

   Class and implementation diagrams

9. **What are the types of behavioral diagrams within UML?**

   Use case, activity, sequence, collaboration, and statechart diagrams

10. **What are some tools that can be used to model with UML?**

    Rational Rose, Visio, whiteboard, pen and paper

Module 2: Use Case Diagrams

1. **What is a good actor name for the person who runs the weekly payroll checks on a payroll system?**

    Payroll Operator

2. **What would be some use cases that would be used in a Payroll system by this actor?**

    Print Weekly Payroll, Add Employee to Payroll, Remove Employee from Payroll, Edit Employee Within Payroll, Change Payroll Amount, Manage Tax Rates

3. **Model a use case diagram for the Paycheck system.**

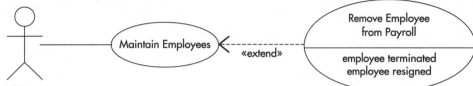

4. **What would be some generalization use cases for the use case Send Letter?**

    Send Notification Letter, Send Late Payment Letter, Send Follow-up Letter

5. **What would be some generalization actors for the actor army personnel?**

    Private, Colonel, Major, Lieutenant, General

6. **What is the difference between an include relationship and an extend relationship?**

    The include relationship is used to indicate that a use case will include functionality from an additional use case to perform its function. The extend relationship indicates that a use case may be extended by another use case.

7. **What would be a valid included use case for the including cases Print Document, Print Envelope, and Print Label?**

    Print

8. **List the extension points that can be used for the following extend relationship.**

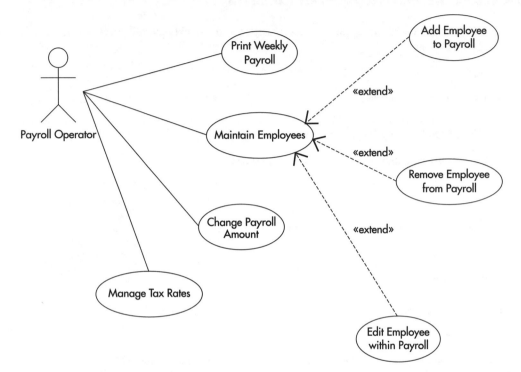

9. **Describe the use case Save Grades as it applied to the grading system used in this module.**

- The student, class, and grades are identified.
- The connection to the database is established.
- The student and class are found in the database.
- The grades are persisted for the student and class.
- The connection to the database is closed.

10. **What are the steps used to create a use case diagram?**

1. Find the actors and use cases.
2. Prioritize the use cases.
3. Detail each use case.
4. Structure the use case model.

Module 3: Introduction to Object-Oriented Design

1. **What is abstraction?**

The generalizing of an item without a type

2. **What is encapsulation?**

The hiding of internal functionality from other components

3. **What is inheritance?**

The gaining (inheriting) of functionality from a parent class

4. **Diagram the generalization of a file. Include three types of files and label the subclasses and superclass.**

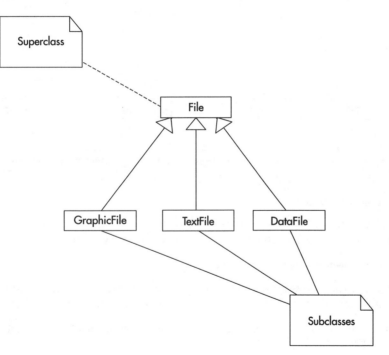

5. **What is multiple inheritance?**

When a single class has more than one superclass

6. **What is hierarchical inheritance?**

When a class is both a subclass and a superclass in the same model

7. **Start with a superclass, Computer Accessory, and diagram three levels of subclasses.**

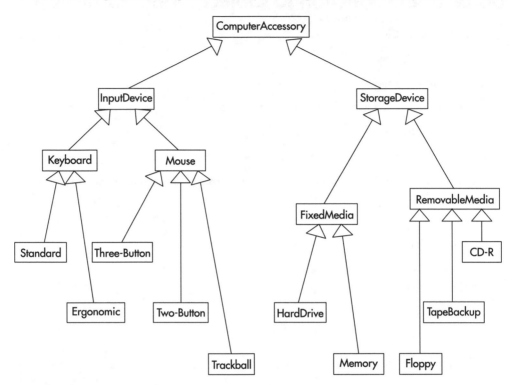

8. **What is polymorphism?**

The ability of two or more abstract classes to have the same interface, but operate on its data differently because each has its own set of code, or way of doing something

9. **How does object-oriented design help code reuse?**

By breaking functionality into normalized units of components, code is neater, easier to locate, and better structured. Each of these characteristics helps promote code reuse.

10. **What are some common functionality or attributes belonging to a hard drive, floppy drive, and CD-ROM drive?**

Read data, file format, size, and speed

Module 4: Workflow Modeling with Activity Diagrams

1. **Model an activity diagram for the use case of a driver starting a car.**

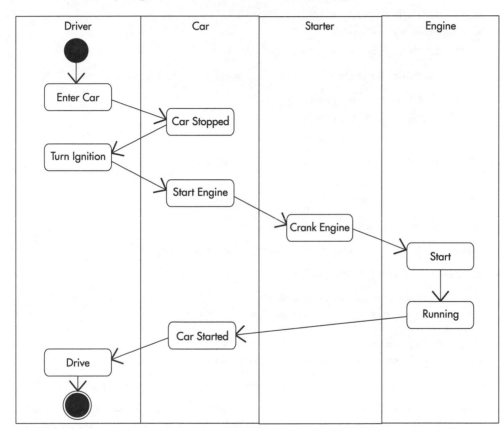

2. **Name some valid states of a file object**

   Open, Closed, Hidden, Visible, Read-Only, Write, Read/Write

3. **What are the notational components of an activity diagram and what are their purposes?**

   - **Activities**   An action state that indicates that something is happening
   - **States**   Indicates that the system has reached a milestone or indicator
   - **Transitions**   Indicate control flow from activities or states to other activities or states

4. What is the difference between guards and triggers?

Guards control the flow of data by evaluating expressions, and triggers force activity to flow in a particular direction by an action.

5. Name the different workflows that might be modeled for the use case of buying a book online.

- User finds the book and purchases it successfully
- User cannot find the book they want
- User finds the book but has trouble purchasing it

6. List some activities for the use case to add an e-mail address to a newsgroup list.

- Check for existence of e-mail address
- Find category for e-mail address
- Add e-mail address to newsgroup

7. What is the difference between using conditions and forks?

Conditions indicate that the control flow will pick a direction, whereas forks indicate that the process will continue in both directions asynchronously (in parallel).

8. What do swim lanes illustrate to the reader?

Swim lanes are used to indicate which object an activity is occurring on.

9. What are the steps to modeling an activity diagram?

1. Identify the business use cases to model.
2. Model the primary paths of each use case.
3. Model all alternative paths.
4. Add swim lanes when necessary.
5. Refine high-level activities into their own activity diagram.

10. What are the advantages of using decision points rather than just guards in an activity model?

Using decision points is helpful when you have more than two resulting control flows because it removes the result from an activity and allows the split to be easily positioned within the diagram to improve readability.

Module 5: Modeling Behavior with Sequence Diagrams

1. Why are sequence diagrams modeled?

Sequence diagrams are used to model object interactions arranged in time sequence and to distribute use case behavior to classes.

2. **What are the four types of messages and what are the differences between them?**

- **Synchronous**   One message cannot start until the previous one completes
- **Return**   Process flow returns to the caller
- **Asynchronous**   Parallel messages do not wait for each other's completion
- **Flat**   The message can either be synchronous or asynchronous (it is not specified)

3. **Model the creation of a database object, the connection of that object to a data source, and the query of the object for a resultset.**

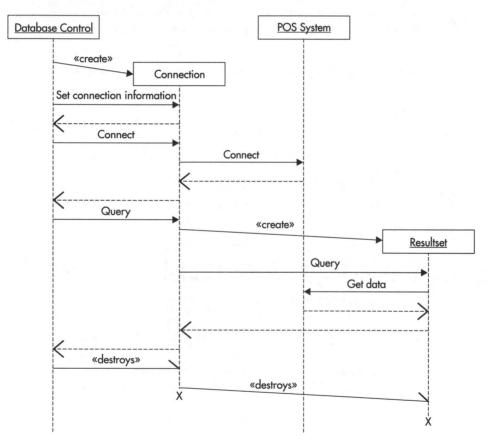

4. **To what do states belong?**

Objects

5. **What are the four steps to modeling a sequence diagram?**

1. Decide on the workflows that you are going to model.
2. Lay out the objects for each model.

3. Include messages and conditions for each model.

4. Draw a single, generic diagram if possible.

6. **What are some differences between use case diagrams and sequence diagrams?**

Use cases are generic, and explain to management and non-technical people what the system will be capable of doing. In many cases, use cases represent the requirements provided by management. Sequence diagrams model the steps that will be taken to achieve each use case within the system.

7. **What is the difference between synchronous and asynchronous messages?**

Synchronous messages force the system to wait until they are finished before executing the next message. Asynchronous messages allow parallel processing because they do not hold up other messages from being executed.

8. **Identify some alternative workflows for taking money out of an ATM machine.**

- The user cannot remember their PIN number
- The ATM cannot verify the PIN number
- The ATM does not have enough money to fulfill the user's request

9. **What are the types of active objects that can be used in a sequence diagram?**

Actors and objects (class instances)

10. **What are the two keywords used when instantiating an object within a sequence diagram?**

«create», «destroys»

Module 6: Defining Domain Models Using Class Diagrams

1. **Model a class diagram to show the association of a Monster scaring a Child.**

2. Add multiplicity to the class diagram you just created to show that a monster always scares at least one child, but never more than eight.

3. Show where a child plays the role of a monster to a parent in a class diagram.

4. Give the parent in your class diagram attributes to indicate their age, sex, and name. Default the age to 21.

5. Give the parent in your class diagram an operation that allows it to kiss its monster (returning success/failure).

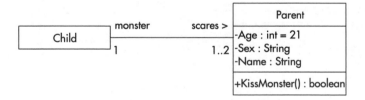

6. **Add a derived attribute to the Parent class called Happy that is true when they successfully kissed their monster.**

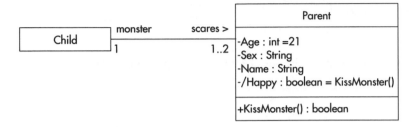

7. **Model an instance of the Parent class, giving it values for its attributes.**

```
Kimberly : Parent
─────────────────────────
-Age : int = 27
-Sex : String = Female
-Name : String = Kimberly
```

8. **Modify your class diagram to indicate the package where any classes or objects come from.**

```
                                    ParentSystem::Parent
                                ──────────────────────────────
   LittleMonsterProgram::Child  -Age : int = 21
   ──────────────┬───  monster   scares >  -Sex : String
                 1            1..2  -Name : String
                                    -/Happy : boolean = KissMonster()
                                ──────────────────────────────
                                    +KissMonster() : boolean
```

9. **What are the steps used to create a class diagram?**

1. Find the classes and their associations.
2. Find the attributes and operations of each class.

10. **What are the two main components of classes?**

- Attributes
- Operations

Module 7: Collaboration Diagrams

1. **Why do we model a collaboration diagram?**

To illustrate the communication between objects or roles

2. **What is the difference between association roles and links?**

Association links relate class roles while links relate objects.

3. **What are the three types of messages and what is each used for?**

- **Synchronous**   Used for sequential messaging (one after another)
- **Asynchronous**   Used for parallel messaging (more than one at a time)
- **Flat**   Used when the type is unknown or unimportant

4. **Model a collaboration diagram to illustrate the communication for dialing a telephone.**

5. **What would be some guard conditions for attempting to send an e-mail message?**

- [address exists] and [no address exists]
- [has attachments] and [does not have attachments]
- [mail server exists] and [mail server does not exist]

6. **How do you model instance creation in a collaboration diagram?**

By sending a creation message to an object instance along a link stereotyped as «create». The created object is stereotyped as «new».

7. **Put the following sequence IDs in order: 1, 1.1, 1.1.1, 1.1.2.1, 1.2.1.2, 1.1.2.2, 1.2.1.1, 1.2.2.2, 1.1.1.1, 1.1.2, 1.2, 1.2.2**

   1
   1.1
   1.2
   1.1.1
   1.1.2
   1.1.1.1
   1.1.2.1
   1.1.2.2
   1.2.1.1
   1.2.1.2
   1.2.2
   1.2.2.2

8. **What is the notation for an object named Kong, of class Server, playing the role of a WebServer?**

   Kong/WebServer:Server

9. **What are the steps required to create a collaboration diagram?**

   1. Identify the elements of the diagram.
   2. Model the structural relationship between those elements.
   3. Model the instance-level diagram.

10. **What are the valid stereotypes for a link in a collaboration diagram?**

    «parameter» and «local»

Module 8: Further Explanation of Class Diagrams

1. **Describe aggregation and composition.**

   Both aggregation and composition are the association relationships used to show whole-part relationships between classes of different objects. Aggregation indicates that the part classes can exist without the whole, while composition indicates the opposite, that part classes cannot exist without the whole.

2. **Model the associations between a Stereo system and its receivers and speakers.**

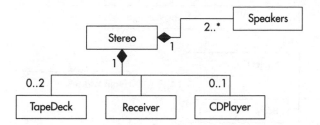

3. **Model the components of an e-mail message with associations.**

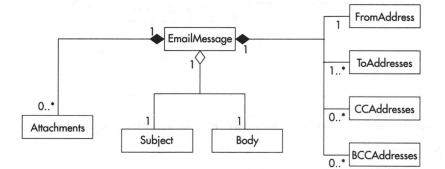

4. **Add navigation to the e-mail message model.**

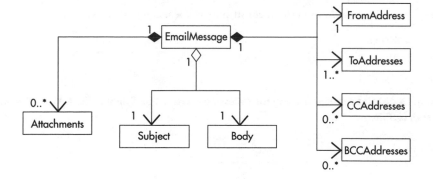

5. Model the e-mail application using graphical containment.

```
┌──────────────────────────────────────────────────┐
│                  EmailMessage                      │
│                                                    │
│  ┌─────────────────────┐                           │
│  │ Subject          1  │   ┌─────────────────────┐ │
│  └─────────────────────┘   │ FromAddress      1  │ │
│                            └─────────────────────┘ │
│  ┌─────────────────────┐                           │
│  │ Body             1  │   ┌─────────────────────┐ │
│  └─────────────────────┘   │ ToAddresses    1..* │ │
│                            └─────────────────────┘ │
│  ┌─────────────────────┐                           │
│  │ Attachments    0..* │   ┌─────────────────────┐ │
│  └─────────────────────┘   │ CCAddresses   0..*  │ │
│                            └─────────────────────┘ │
│                            ┌─────────────────────┐ │
│                            │ BCCAddresses  0..*  │ │
│                            └─────────────────────┘ │
│                                                    │
└──────────────────────────────────────────────────┘
```

6. What are the four types of generalization constraints you learned in this module?

- Incomplete
- Complete
- Disjoint
- Overlapping

7. What are the types of composition constraints you learned in this module?

- Ordering
- Sorting
- Navigation

8. Model a disjoint constraint using the following classes: File, Binary, Text, WordDocument, and DatabaseFile.

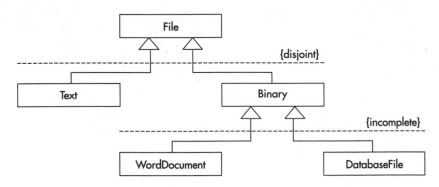

9. **What is the difference between a constraint and a discriminator?**

Generalization *constraints* are used to indicate that the generalization has a condition associated with it. *Discriminators* are used to indicate what role a generalization relationship is playing for the two involved classes.

10. **What are some examples of predefined constraints?**

- Incomplete constraint
- Complete constraint
- Disjoint constraint
- Overlapping constraint
- Ordered constraint
- Sorted constraint

Module 9: Further Explanation of Sequence Diagramming

1. **What are some messages that would be sent during a phone call from a Telephone object and a SwitchBoard object?**

- Telephone sends RequestDialTone message to SwitchBoard
- Telephone sends ButtonPressed message to SwitchBoard
- Telephone sends Conversation message to SwitchBoard
- Telephone sends HangUp message to SwitchBoard

2. **What are some messages that would be sent during a phone call from a SwitchBoard object to a Telephone object?**

- SwitchBoard sends DialTone message
- SwitchBoard sends Ring message
- SwitchBoard sends HangUp message to SwitchBoard
- SwitchBoard sends CallerIDInformation to SwitchBoard

3. **What are some recursive calls that a Telephone object may encounter during a phone call?**

- ResetPhone
- ProgramPhone
- PlayMessages

4. **Model a phone call using time constraints.**

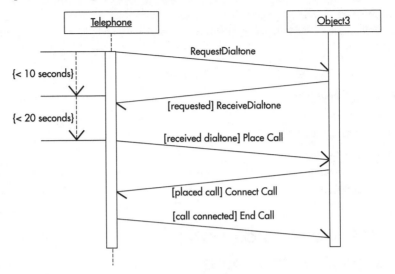

5. **How is iteration modeled?**

With a rectangle surrounding the messages that are iterated and a guard expression in the bottom-right corner of the rectangle

6. **Model a phone call using iteration.**

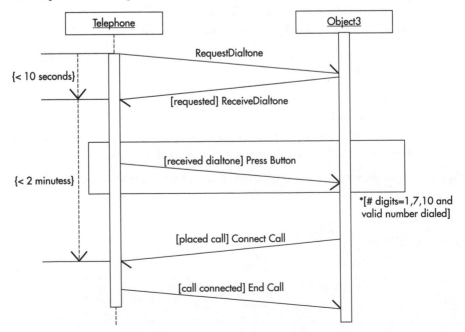

7. **When an object's lifeline is not visible, because it is obstructed by its control rectangle, what is inferred?**

That the object is involved in the entire sequence of messages modeled in the current sequence diagram

8. **What is a good comment for the phone call diagram that you have created?**

After a dial tone is received, the Telephone can send the ButtonPress message to the SwitchBoard until a valid number is constructed that is one digit (0), seven digits (local number), or ten digits (long distance number).

9. **How are changes in time modeled for messages?**

With messages sloping from the calling object to the object that is called

10. **How is time duration modeled?**

Using construction marks to show a time duration between two or more messages

Module 10: Modeling Behavior with Statechart Diagrams

1. **What are the basic notational components of statechart diagrams?**

States and transitions

2. **What is the difference between statechart diagrams and activity diagrams?**

Statechart diagrams model behavior that changes the state of a single entity, whereas activity diagrams model behavior among different entities.

3. **What does synchronization accomplish in statechart diagrams?**

Allows more than one state to be valid at a time

4. **What is the difference between events and actions?**

Events are behaviors that cause states to change, whereas actions are behaviors that occur as a result of an event.

5. **What are the steps involved in diagramming a statechart diagram?**

1. Identify the entities that need to be further detailed.
2. Identify the start and end states for each entity.
3. Determine the events relating to each entity.
4. Create the statechart diagram beginning with the start event.
5. Create composite states where necessary.

6. **What is a substate?**

Another statechart diagram that applies to a particular state, ultimately allowing that state to have another state that better describes its particular state

7. How is a composite state modeled?

As a large state with the substate diagram embedded inside of it

8. What are the five basic types of actions?

Entry, Exit, Do, Include, and Event

9. What are the two different notations for actions?

The two notations for actions are as follows:

```
action-label / action

event-name (parameters) [guard-condition] / action
```

10. What are decision points used for?

To serve as a point for transitions to originate when many transitions should originate from a state

Module 11: Architecting with Implementation Diagrams

1. What is the difference between a component and a deployment diagram?

Component diagrams illustrate relationships between pieces of software, while deployment diagrams illustrate relationships between pieces of hardware.

2. What do components represent?

Source code, binaries, executables, scripts, or command files

3. What are the relationships between components called?

Dependencies

4. What is the purpose of modeling contained components?

To illustrate that a component consists of other components

5. What do nodes represent?

Hardware

6. What are the relationships between nodes called?

Communication associations

7. List the steps to create an implementation diagram.

1. Add nodes.
2. Add communication associations.

3. Add components, classes, and objects.

4. Add dependencies.

8. What is meant by stereotyping dependencies?

A dependency can be stereotyped to give meaning to the relationship.

9. List some nodes that can be found in your home network.

- HomePC
- CableModem
- Printer
- Scanner

10. List some components of a client server application.

- DataAccess
- BusinessObject
- DesktopInterface
- WebInterface
- HandheldInterface

Module 12: Using the Object Constraint Language

1. What are the three stereotypes of a constraint and what is the context of each?

- «pre-condition» (operations)
- «post-condition» (operations)
- «invariant» (classes)

2. List the operations used for Integers.

=, < >, <, >, <=, >=, +, -, *, /, max( ) or min( ), mod( ), div( ), abs, round, and floor

3. List the operations used for Reals.

=, < >, <, >, <=, >=, +, -, *, /, max( ) or min( ), abs, round, and floor

4. List the operations used for Booleans.

or, and, xor, and < >

5. List the operations used for Strings.

concat( ), =, < >, size, toLower, and toUpper

6. **What are the three types of collections in OCL and what are the differences?**

   - Set (a distinct list of items that is unordered)
   - Sequence (a list of items that is ordered and allows repetition)
   - Bag (an unordered list of items that also allows repetition)

7. **List some operations used for all types of collections.**

   select, reject, forall, exists, size, count, isEmpty

8. **Evaluate** `(bag{True, False, True, False})->union(bag{True})`

   `(bag{True, False, True, False})->union(bag{True}) = bag{True, False}`

9. **Evaluate** `sequence{'zachary', 'kimberly', 'jason'})->last`

   `(sequence{'zachary', 'kimberly', 'jason'})->last = 'jason'`

10. **Evaluate** `(set{'jason', 'rocks'})->excluding('rolls')`

    `(set{'jason', 'rocks'})->excluding('rolls') = set{'jason', 'rocks'}`

11. **Evaluate** `(set{True, false})->including(True)`

    `(set{True, false})->including(True) = True`

12. **Evaluate** `(set{'jason', 'rocks'})->excluding('rocks')`

    `(set{'jason', 'rocks'})->excluding('rocks') = set({'jason'})`

13. **Evaluate** `(set{1, 2})->union(set{0})`

    `(set{1, 2})->union(set{0}) = bag{0, 1, 2}`

14. **Evaluate** `sequence{'zachary', 'kimberly', 'jason'})->first`

    `(sequence{'zachary', 'kimberly', 'jason'})->first = sequence{'zachary'}`

15. **Evaluate** `(sequence{1, 2, 2, 3, 0})->last`

    `(sequence{1, 2, 2, 3, 0})->last = 0`

16. **Evaluate** `sequence{1, 2, 3, 4})->append(sequence{5})`

    `(sequence{1, 2, 3, 4})->append(sequence{5}) = sequence{5, 1, 2, 3, 4}`

17. **Evaluate** `bag{'jason', 'jason', 'jason'})->asSet`

    `(bag{'jason', 'jason', 'jason'})->asSet = set{'jason'}`

18. **Evaluate** `(bag{True, False, True, False})->intersection(bag{True})`

    `(bag{True, False, True, False})->intersection(bag{True}) = set(True)`

Glossary

Presented here is a set of brief definitions of the major terms you will encounter in this book. Every attempt has been made to ensure that all of the important terms have been included.

abstraction   The method of creating general items that suppress unnecessary details, to focus on a specific set of details that are of interest to the system being modeled.

action states   States that represent atomic actions such as an operation.

actions   Used to represent procedures that usually change the state of the system.

activation   The time that an object has focus in a sequence diagram.

activity   Something that a role may be asked to perform.

activity diagram   Used to analyze the behavior within more complex use cases and show their interaction with each other. Activity diagrams are very similar to statechart diagrams in that they represent a flow of data; however, activity diagrams are used to model business workflows during the design of use cases in the analysis phase of modeling, whereas statechart diagrams are used to represent objects in the design phase. Activity diagrams are usually used to represent the more complicated business activities, helping you identify use cases or the interaction between and within the use cases.

actor   Used to represent something that uses your system; can be a person or another system, and is depicted by a stick figure with the actor's role name listed below it.

aggregation   Used to illustrate the whole-part relationship between two classes where one class is considered a whole, made up of one or more classes comprising its parts. In an aggregation, the part classes can exist without the whole, but when they are aggregated to a whole, they are used to comprise that class.

alternative flow   A flow in a sequence or activity diagram that is taken due to a branch or a condition.

analysis   The process that is taken when dealing with a domain expert to learn about the system and ultimately model it to describe what the system does.

append OCL operation   Adds data to the beginning of a sequence collection.

asSet OCL operation   Removes the duplicates from a bag collection.

association   A relationship that models a bidirectional relationship between items.

association role   A relationship between two classes' roles.

asynchronous messages   Messages that are sent from an active object, but to which the active object doesn't await a response.

attribute   Contains the state data for a class when it is instantiated as an object.

bag OCL collection   An unordered list of items that also allows repetition.

base class   *See* superclass.

behavioral diagram   Used to show how process flows between components, classes, users, and the system. There are five behavioral diagrams belonging to UML: use case, activity, sequence, collaboration, and statechart.

black box   Something that has known functionality but the means in which this functionality is carried out is unknown. The functionality of an object is hidden, with encapsulation, from all other objects.

Boolean (OCL)   A value that is either true or false.

branches   Means for a sequence or activity diagram to change its control flow based upon particular conditions.

class   A representation of a generalized thing, such as an animal, a person, a car, a ticket, or a system. It is a description of a set of objects that share the same members (attributes, operations, methods, and relationships).

class diagram   Used to represent the different underlying pieces (classes), their relationship to each other, and which subsystem they belong to.

collaboration diagram   Used to represent the interaction and the relationships between the objects created in earlier steps of your domain modeling process; can also be used to model messages between different objects, and how their advance associations can be used to navigate the model.

collection (OCL)   A group of items that are somehow related, possibly sorted and ordered, and possibly having business rules associated with them to enforce which type of items are allowed in the collection.

communication association   Used to relate nodes of an implementation diagram to each other. This relationship identifies that the two pieces of hardware communicate with each other by some means.

complete constraint   Indicates that all possible generalized classes are shown.

component   A single piece of software. It can be a file, product, executable, script, or so on. It is a replaceable part of a system that packages the implementation of the realization of a set of interfaces.

component diagram   Used to illustrate how components of a system interact with each other. It would show dependencies between source files and classes as well as which components they belong to.

composite states   An alternative means to model substates by creating a large state that has individual states within it.

composition association   An association relationship between two classes in which the whole class is made up of the part classes, and the part classes need the whole class to exist.

composition graphical containment   Used as an alternative means to model composition by modeling a large box with all of the composite part classes contained inside.

construction phase   Phase of the Unified Process that is the actual building of the product from the design of the system.

context   Indicates what item is being constrained. The constraint itself acts like an expression so that it evaluates to a specific type (such as a number or a True or False value).

control rectangles   Modeled to indicate general focus of control or to specify activation phases.

count OCL operation   Returns the number of items in the collection that are equivalent to the item passed to the operation.

«create» stereotype   Indicates that a new object is instantiated.

decision points   Make the diagram more visually appealing by grouping transitions in a focal point away from the state from which they will go in their own direction, which is a convenience when modeling statechart diagrams. Decision points, for all practical purposes, do the same thing as ordinary guards do, but they do it more neatly, especially if you have a large diagram with a lot of different conditions.

dependencies   Used to illustrate relationships between two components. Changing the independent element of the relationship will affect the dependent element.

deployment diagram   Models where components will wind up after they are installed on systems and how the systems interact with each other. Deployment diagrams are modeled to illustrate relationships between hardware.

derived attributes   Attributes that are calculated automatically based upon math, string functions, or some other business logic.

derived class   *See* subclass.

«destroys» stereotype   Indicates that the associated object is being destroyed.

discriminator   Used to indicate what role a generalization relationship is playing for the two involved classes; indicates to the reader the role of the subclass in the generalization association as it applies to the related superclass.

disjoint constraint   Indicates that the generalized classes immediately below the constraint cannot be subclassed with common clauses.

do action   Used to specify the activity that occurs while the state is being occupied.

domain expert   The person who is considered to be an authority of the system you will be creating.

duration constraint   Indicates the maximum time within which a group of messages can execute.

elaboration phase   The phase of the Unified Process in which the design takes place. During this phase, you evolve the use cases discovered in the inception phase into a design of the domain, its subsystems, and the business objects related to it. From there, you iteratively turn this domain model into a software design using more detailed diagrams that will eventually model classes and their members.

encapsulation   The method of stuffing an item with the functionality and data that pertain to it. Encapsulation is the characteristic of object-oriented design that says that how a class operates is nobody's business but its own.

end state   The last state in an activity diagram.

entry action   Used to specify the action that occurs when the state has been entered.

event action   Used to specify the action that occurs when a particular event has fired.

events   Used to indicate what triggers a transition.

excluding OCL operation   Removes an item from the set if it exists.

exists OCL operation   Evaluates to True if at least one item in the collection satisfies the expression.

exit action   Used to specify the action that occurs when the state is being abandoned for another.

«extends» stereotype   Used to indicate that one use case may be extended by another.

first OCL operation   Retrieves the first items in the sequence.

flat messages   Indicate that no distinction is made between synchronous and asynchronous messaging.

forall OCL operation   Returns a Boolean value of True if every element in the collection satisfies an expression.

forks   Allow parallel processes to begin.

generalization   A technique that is used to indicate inheritance of an item. This relationship indicates that one element is more general and the other is more specific. The more specific item is fully compatible with the more general and an instance of it can be used to replace the more general.

generalization constraints   Used to indicate that the generalization has a condition associated with it.

graphical containment of components   Modeling components inside other components to indicate that the components are contained within the other components.

guard   A guard is noted on a transition between two activities, states, and messages. A guard is enclosed in brackets (for example, [guardname]) and is used to allow the control to flow only in a direction that meets a prerequisite.

guillemets (« ... »)   Characters that are used when indicating a stereotype.

implementation diagram   Used to show where the physical components of a system are going to be placed in relation to each other, the hardware, or the Internet. Component and deployment diagrams are the two types of implementation diagrams.

inception phase   The phase of the Unified Process in which you do your analysis. You discuss with the software matter expert (or domain expert) what the system you will be designing should do. In this stage, the business requirements need to be identified, fleshed out, and modeled in use case diagrams.

include action   Invokes a submachine, represented by another statechart diagram.

«includes» stereotype   Used to indicate that a use case will include functionality from an additional use case to perform its function.

including OCL operation   Appends the new item to the set if it doesn't already exist.

incomplete constraint   Indicates that the list of generalized or subclassed classes is not complete.

incremental-iterative software lifecycle method   Divides a project into subprojects, and allows you to perform the waterfall method on each. Instead of completing functionality in the entire application with each pass, as with the iterative method, the iterative-incremental method completes components based upon functionality with each phase.

Integer (OCL)   Any whole number (without a fraction), such as 3, 2, 1, 0, −1, −2, and −3. Integers can be Real numbers but Real numbers cannot be Integers.

intersection OCL operation   Produces a set that contains only the items common to both bags.

«invariant» stereotype   Indicates that the attributes must remain true throughout the lifetime of the system.

isEmpty OCL operation   Returns True if the collection has no items in it.

iterative (spiral) software lifecycle method   *See* spiral (iterative) software lifecycle method.

joins   Allow parallel processes to catch up and resume a single-process flow.

last OCL operation   Retrieves the last items in the sequence.

lifeline   Used to illustrate what is happening to an object in a chronological fashion.

link   The relationship between two objects.

«local» stereotype   Indicates that the object has local scope as a variable within the other object.

messages   Used to illustrate communication between different active objects of a sequence diagram.

multiple inheritance   The situation in which a class inherits functionality from more than one other class.

multiplicity   A single number or a range of numbers, indicating how many objects of that class relate to one object of another class. The use of a single number means that there is always exactly that number of objects of that class, such as 1, 2, or 3.

node   Used to represent a piece of hardware, whether it is a printer, computer, scanner, or telephone pole.

note   An area on the diagram where you can enter comments.

object   An instance of a class with its own set of data (a class with state).

Object Constraint Language (OCL)   A means of indicating limitations within your modeled system. It is an optional addition to UML that can be used to better define the behavior of your objects. With OCL, one can define attributes such as minimum, maximum, default, and acceptable ranges for data that the system will use.

object diagram   Very similar to a class diagram, except instead of dealing with classes, it shows objects that are instances of classes. Object diagrams are usually more about design by example. In other words, objects deal with individual unique things where classes are more generic.

Object Management Group (OMG)   A group of over 800 software vendors, developers, and end users dedicated to the promotion of object technology used in developing distributed computing systems. OMG (www.omg.org) is a nonprofit consortium providing common frameworks for object-oriented applications to build upon.

object-oriented analysis (OOA)   The process that is used to attempt to understand (analyze) a system using classes and objects for the world relating to the system. It is the process of creating a vocabulary to describe the system that is to be modeled.

object-oriented design (OOD)   The method used to record the vocabulary found in the analysis phase. It gives the model behavior that is required for the system to exist.

object-oriented programming (OOP)   The actual implementation of the model created in the object-oriented design.

operations   Used to provide functionality to a class when it is instantiated as an object.

ordered constraint   Used to indicate that the objects of one class are related to the object of the other class in a particular order.

overlapping constraint   Acts as the disjoint constraint's opposite; shows to the reader that the two subclassed classes share a common subclass.

packages   A way of grouping elements into common categories. Packages can even contain other packages.

parameter list   A group of variables that are sent along with the call to the operation.

«parameter» stereotype   Indicates that the object is a parameter of the other object.

polymorphism   The ability of two or more abstract classes to have the same interface, but operate on its data differently because each has its own set of code, or way of doing something.

«post-condition» stereotype   A value that needs to be True before the context of a constraint can be considered complete.

«pre-condition» stereotype   A value that needs to be True before the context of a constraint can be realized.

prepend OCL operation   Adds data to the end of a sequence.

private attributes   Used only by the class that they belong to. They usually are included in order to provide functionality and data that will ultimately be exposed by a public member of the class interface.

procedural design   Entails every function accessing one another without boundaries.

protected attributes   Visible to classes of the same system. Classes outside of the current system cannot access protected attributes.

public attributes   Visible to any class.

Rational Rose   One of the first complete UML packages to hit the market. Although pricey in many situations, Rational Rose is an all-in-one package that allows you to reverse-engineer your code into models, change your models, and then update your code to reflect the changes.

Rational Software Corporation   The company that produced Rational Rose. Rational Software is extremely involved in the standardization of UML, and hired all three of the original UML contributors.

Rational Unified Process (RUP)   *See* Unified Process.

Real (OCL)   Any number (with or without a fraction) such as 3.0, 2.34, 1.1, 0.0, −1.5, and −2.45. Integers can be Real numbers but Real numbers cannot be Integers.

reject OCL operation   Returns the collection that is composed of items that evaluate to False when compared to the given expression.

relationships   The associations that link elements.

return message   Shows that control flow has returned to the calling active object, and that the synchronous message has completed its operation.

role   Used to illustrate what the first class does for the second class.

select OCL operation   Produces a collection based upon a given criteria. It returns the same type of collection that is passed to it.

sequence diagram   Used to show interaction between actors and objects and other objects. Messages are sent from actor to object, object to object, and object to actor to show the flow of control through a system. Sequence diagrams are used to realize use cases by documenting how a use case is solved with the current design of the system. Sequence diagrams model the interaction between high-level class instances, detailing where process control is at every stage of the communication process. Sequence diagrams can be used to show every possible path through an interaction, or show a single path through an interaction.

sequence OCL collection   A list of items that is ordered and that allows repetition.

sequencing   The act of indicating the order in which messages are sent.

set OCL collection   A distinct list of items that is unordered.

size OCL operation   Returns the number of items in the collection.

sorted constraint   Indicates that the objects of the class are sorted when related to the other object of the other class in the association.

spaghetti code   A term for code in which the lines of operation are tangled because any piece of functionality can call any other piece of functionality.

spiral (iterative) software lifecycle method   Starts with analysis, continues with design, follows up with implementation, and then repeats itself by returning to the analysis phase. This method allows the development team to progressively complete a project.

start state   The first state in a model.

state   A snapshot or a milestone of an object's behavior at a particular point in time.

statechart diagram   Used to represent a single object and how its behavior causes it to change state. Very similar to a well-known state machine model, the statechart diagram is used during the crossover between the analysis and design phases. A statechart diagram is a wonderful way to visualize the flow of an application.

string (OCL)   Any value that includes any amount of text data such as "Jason Rocks" or "a".

structural diagrams   The two types of diagrams that are considered structural are class diagrams and implementation diagrams. Within these two categories, we can find four specific types of diagrams (class, object, component, and deployment diagrams). This type of diagram is used to represent physical components of a system.

subclass   A class that is a part of another whole class (superclass).

substates   States that are unique only to another state; states that are part of a composite state.

subsystems   Pieces of a larger system, sometimes broken into their own system for ease of modeling, development, or implementation.

superclass   A base class that other classes are derived from.

swim lanes   Used to isolate activities according to their domain, or object.

synchronization bars   Used in a statechart diagram to show where states need to catch up with or wait for others. Synchronization bars are used to show concurrent states.

synchronous message   Indicates that flow is interrupted until the message has completed and any messages sent from that message have completed.

system   Something that performs a function.

time constraint   A constraint that indicates the maximum time within which a single message can execute.

transition phase   The phase of the Unified Process that deals with delivering the product to customers, perhaps a beta site or even the actual client.

transitions   Used to show flow from one state to another.

triggers   Used to move control from one action to another.

Unified Modeling Language (UML)   A language used to model a system.

Unified Process   The Unified Modeling Language is only a language. It is not a way of designing a system, but rather a way to model a system. To use UML, you need to apply a method to it. A number of methods have been designed, but the most popular, and probably the first to deal with UML, is the Rational Unified Process (RUP), also called the Unified Process.

union OCL operation   Adds all the occurrences of one set to another.

use case   A single thing that an actor does with the system. A use case is a description of the system's behavior that results in a particular value for the actor. Use cases can be used to diagram the main flow of events in a system, for when there are no errors. They can also be used to diagram alternative flows (related directly to error-handling situations).

use case diagram   Contains use cases and actors, illustrating the relationships between the two sets. Use case diagrams are the starting point of the analysis phase when designing a system. Originally invented by Ivar Jacobson, use cases are the foundation of a use case diagram. They are joined by associations and linked to actors in order to project the overall structure of a system to nontechnical readers such as management and end users.

Visio   A software application developed by Visio Corporation (now owned by Microsoft) that enables users to create graphical models, charts, and diagrams. Since its inception, Visio has come a long way with the UML functionality it offers. An object manager has been added, which offers component management similar to that found in Rational Rose. The objects that you create in one diagram can easily be migrated to other diagrams by simply dragging and dropping them.

waterfall software lifecycle method   The most straightforward of the different software lifecycle methods, it consists of first performing analysis, then design, and then development in a strong sequence.

whole-part relationship   The relationship between classes in which one class is made of, or consists of, other classes.

Index

Q

R

INTERNATIONAL CONTACT INFORMATION

AUSTRALIA
McGraw-Hill Book Company
Australia Pty. Ltd.
TEL +61-2-9900-1800
FAX +61-2-9878-8881
http://www.mcgraw-hill.com.au
books-it_sydney@mcgraw-hill.com

CANADA
McGraw-Hill Ryerson Ltd.
TEL +905-430-5000
FAX +905-430-5020
http://www.mcgraw-hill.ca

**GREECE, MIDDLE EAST, & AFRICA
(Excluding South Africa)**
McGraw-Hill Hellas
TEL +30-210-6560-990
TEL +30-210-6560-993
TEL +30-210-6560-994
FAX +30-210-6545-525

MEXICO (Also serving Latin America)
McGraw-Hill Interamericana Editores
S.A. de C.V.
TEL +525-1500-5108
FAX +525-117-1589
http://www.mcgraw-hill.com.mx
carlos_ruiz@mcgraw-hill.com

SINGAPORE (Serving Asia)
McGraw-Hill Book Company
TEL +65-6863-1580
FAX +65-6862-3354
http://www.mcgraw-hill.com.sg
mghasia@mcgraw-hill.com

SOUTH AFRICA
McGraw-Hill South Africa
TEL +27-11-622-7512
FAX +27-11-622-9045
robyn_swanepoel@mcgraw-hill.com

SPAIN
McGraw-Hill/
Interamericana de España, S.A.U.
TEL +34-91-180-3000
FAX +34-91-372-8513
http://www.mcgraw-hill.es
professional@mcgraw-hill.es

**UNITED KINGDOM, NORTHERN,
EASTERN, & CENTRAL EUROPE**
McGraw-Hill Education Europe
TEL +44-1-628-502500
FAX +44-1-628-770224
http://www.mcgraw-hill.co.uk
emea_queries@mcgraw-hill.com

ALL OTHER INQUIRIES Contact:
McGraw-Hill/Osborne
TEL +1-510-420-7700
FAX +1-510-420-7703
http://www.osborne.com
omg_international@mcgraw-hill.com